The 1/4th [illegible] e) Battn., York and [illegible] egiment, 1914 - 1919.

by

Captain D. P. GRANT, M.C., M.A.

Printed for private circulation
by
THE ARDEN PRESS
STAMFORD STREET
LONDON, S.E.1

Printed and bound by Antony Rowe Ltd, Eastbourne

PREFACE

THIS book has been written chiefly because certain officers, who for various reasons have had to sever their connection with the Hallamshires, felt that many like themselves would wish to be reminded—more and more as the years go by—of their experiences with the Battalion during the War.

It will be obvious that few, if any, are qualified to write the History of the Hallamshires from first-hand experience, and I hasten to make it clear that my task has been to some extent that of editor. It is my pleasant duty to acknowledge the generosity of several officers—particularly Captains Ryan and Elrington—for allowing me to revise their contributions to the book, so as to make the latter more uniform in plan. My thanks are due, too, to Colonel Branson for allowing me to consult maps, diaries, etc., in possession of the Battalion, and for his criticism and help in many other ways; to the Geographical Section, General Staff, the War Office for their courtesy and help in the matter of maps for the book; to the Controller of H.M. Stationery Office for permission to print extracts from Sir D. Haig's Despatches and to reproduce the maps; to Messrs. Methuen & Co., Ltd., for permission to quote from Professor A. F. Pollard's "A Short History of the Great War"; and to Messrs. Nelson & Sons, Ltd., for permission to quote a short extract from Nelson's "History of the War."

At the same time, the responsibility for the opinions expressed in the book, as well as for its shortcomings, is mine. In this connection it is hoped that the excellent 1/100000 maps (which we knew so well during the war), with parts of the approximate Allied Lines superimposed, will be found sufficient for ordinary purposes; to have included more elaborate maps and illustrations would have increased the cost of the book enormously, thus defeating one of our objects in publishing it.

D. P. GRANT.

Harsnetts,
Chigwell,
Essex.

FOREWORD

THIS modest record of the services of the First Hallamshires in the Great War adds yet another page to the glorious history of the York and Lancaster Regiment.

I had the honour of joining the 49th West Riding Division on September 20th, 1915. Early in June, 1916, I took over the command of the 148th Infantry Brigade, when I had the privilege of having the 1/4th (Hallamshire) Battalion, York and Lancaster Regt. under my command until October 28th, 1917.

I feel that this work needs little introduction or explanation from me to those who served in the Hallamshires, or are connected with it. It is right that the deeds of this gallant Battalion should live in story, not merely as a memorial of what the soldiers of all ranks serving in it accomplished, but as an example for all time of the spirit in which the dangers and hardships of the greatest war in history were met by the Hallamshire men, and as an inspiration for those who come after, who in their turn may be called upon to play the game as it was played by those who went before them.

It is impossible to describe the realities of this war so as to bring more than a faint image of them to the minds of those who have not actually witnessed them; it is impossible to realise adequately the courage, devotion to duty, determination and endurance of these men in the front line, who went through and surmounted these realities, triumphantly and cheerily.

This story can only give a bare outline of the individual and collective deeds of gallantry of the Hallamshires, but it will recall the memory of many long days and nights in the trenches, of duty done by all ranks in all places, of many hours spent in digging, of patrols, wiring parties, carrying parties, of days passed under shell, machine-gun and rifle fire, of raids by night and attacks by day, of a stubborn defence, a glorious advance, and the final overthrow of the enemy after days, months and years devoted to the service of King and Country. It is a narrative of the adventures in training-camps, in billets, in trenches, in battles and in periods of rest, of that splendid body of men known as the Territorial Armies, which came into being in 1908 from the old Volunteer Force.

The 49th West Riding Division, of which the Hallamshires formed a part, was one of the first four divisions to go to France after the Regular Army had embarked, and they were able to hold the fort during a period when no other troops were available. Certainly no other force had so much spade work as the force which the Hallamshires represented. How well the work was done is shown in this story of comradeship, endeavour and sacrifice in the great cause.

By far the greater part deals with periods of trench warfare—largely in the Ypres Salient; but during 1916-1917 the Battalion was more often severely tried in battle. The Somme, Nieuport, Passchendaele, stand out as landmarks of the greatest difficulties and hardships which the Hallamshires overcame and carried through with that undaunted spirit which characterized the Battalion from its gallant Commander downwards. How much of the Hallamshire spirit was due to Colonel Douglas Branson's personality is well known to his superiors and subordinates.

It was perhaps at Passchendaele that the Hallamshires gained most distinction. The hardships caused by adverse weather and indescribable mud, with scanty artillery support, brought out all the cheerful qualities and unfailing spirit which were so marked among them, enabling them, by strenuous attack, to relieve the pressure on our Allies further South, and again, after only four days' rest, not only to relieve the Australians opposite Passchendaele, but by night advances to push forward their line. So great was this success that on relief by the 50th Canadian Division on October 23rd, I received a letter of thanks and congratulation from the Canadian Corps Commander for the progress made towards the Canadian objectives. Their cheerful spirit at this time under adverse conditions of weather and heavy artillery fire was most remarkable.

It is well that such stories should be told to the survivors of the events, the tale of the great days and great friendships be handed on. To future generations of the Hallamshire lads let them be an inspiration!

R. L. ADLERCRON,

Brigadier-General.

CONTENTS.

I
BELGIUM 1:100.000
HAZEBR
Gravelines
Bergues
Bourbourg
Audruicq
Watten
CASSEL
ST. OMER
FORÊT D'EPERLECQUES
FORÊT DE CLAIRMARAIS
Wormhoudt
Wylder
Esquelbecq
Bollezeele
Volkerinckhove
Zegerscappel
Drincham
Eringhem
Crochte
Socx
Quaedypre
Hondschoote
Oye
Offekerque
Nortkerque
Clairmarais
Tournehem
Nordausque
Moringhem
Zutkerque
Millain
Merckeghem
Rubrouck
Ledringhem
Arneke
Ochtezeele
Zermezeele
Bavinchove
Steenvoorde
Buysscheure
St. Momelin
Salperwick
Tilques
Serques
Houlle
Moulle
Eperlecques
Ruminghem
Looberghe
Brouckerque
Craywick
Cappelle
Coudekerque
Warhem
Loon-Plage
Vieille Eglise
Nle. Eglise
St. Omer Capelle
St. Folquin
Zuytpeene
Noordpeene
Hardifort
Wemaers Cappel
Staple
Zudausques
Tatinghem
Bonningues
Quercamps
Guemy
Zouafques
Recques
Nielles

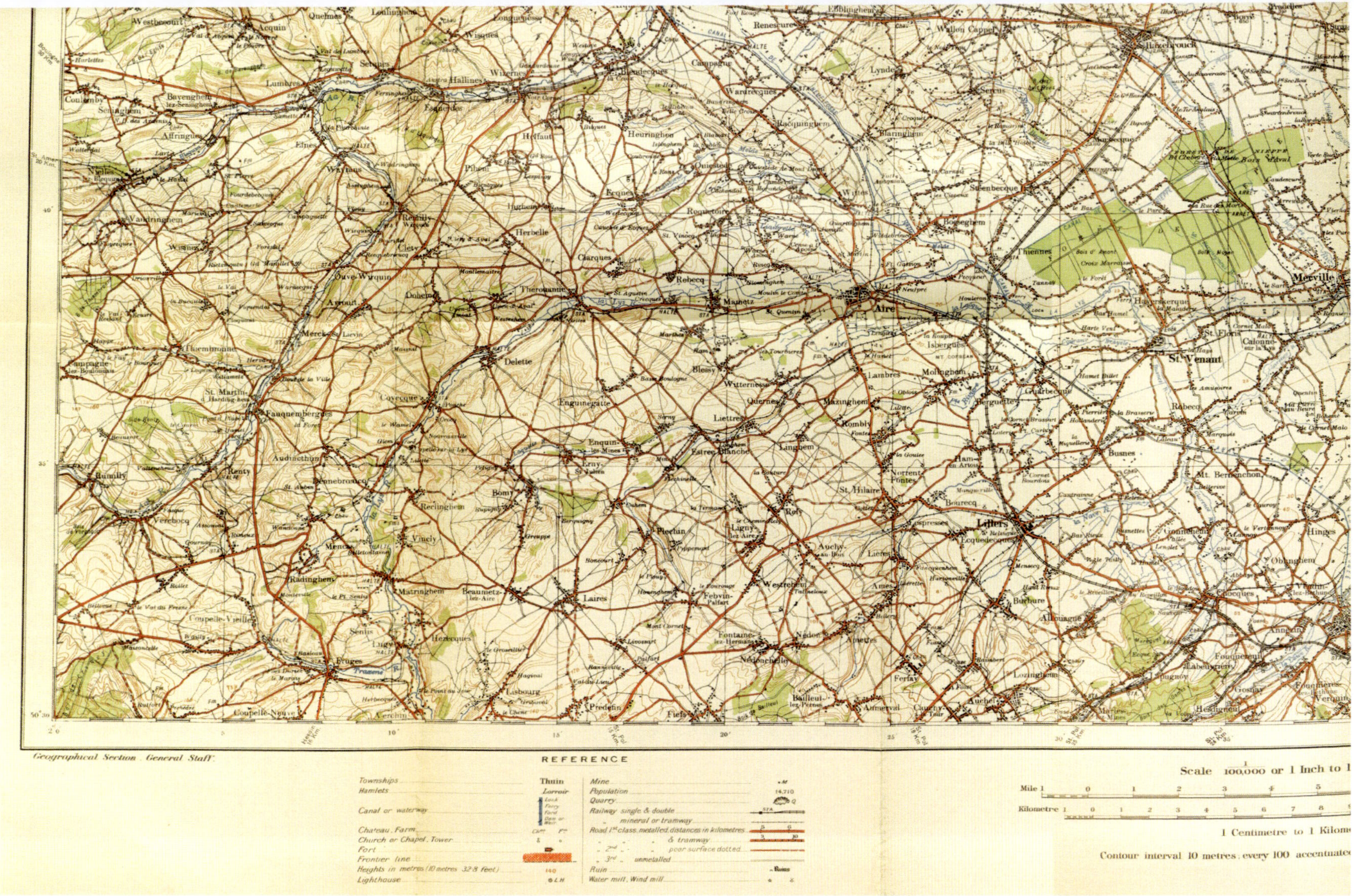
Geographical Section. General Staff.
REFERENCE
Townships
Thuin
Hamlets
Lorroir
Canal or waterway
Chateau, Farm
Church or Chapel, Tower
Fort
Frontier line
Heights in metres (10 metres 32·8 feet)
140
Lighthouse
Mine
Population
14,710
Quarry
Railway single & double
mineral or tramway
Road 1st class metalled distances in kilometres
& tramway
2nd
poor surface dotted
3rd
unmetalled
Ruin
Water mill, Wind mill
Scale 1/100,000 or 1 Inch to 1
Mile
Kilometre
1 Centimetre to 1 Kilom
Contour interval 10 metres, every 100 accentuated
Hazebrouck
Merville
Aire
St. Venant
Lillers
Thérouanne
Fauquembergues
Fruges
Delette
Rebecq
Lumbres
Renty
Rumilly
Laires
Auchel
Hinges
Lambres
Isbergues
Busnes
Blessy
Wittes
Enquin-les-Mines
Estrée Blanche
Lières
Ames
Febvin-Palfart
Heuringhem
Ecques
Campagne
Wardrecques
Racquinghem
Blaringhem
Steenbecque
Thiennes
Mazinghem
Lambres
Lynde
Renescure
Wallon Cappel
Westbecourt
Acquin
Setques
Wisques
Wizernes
Blendecques
Hallines
Esquerdes
Affringues
Bayenghem lez-Seninghem
Coulomby
Seninghem
Elnes
Wavrans
Remilly-Wirquin
Cléty
Ouve-Wirquin
Herbelle
Clarques
Dohem
Avroult
Merck St. Lievin
Thiembronne
Audincthun
Coyecque
Bomy
Reclinghem
Vincly
Matringhem
Beaumetz-lez-Aire
Radinghem
Senlis
Lugy
Hezecques
Coupelle-Vieille
Coupelle-Neuve
Predefin
Fiefs
Nedon
Nedonchel
Bailleul-lez-Pernes
Amettes
Auchy-au-Bois
Westrehem
Ligny-lez-Aire
Pippemont
Rely
Linghem
St. Hilaire
Norrent-Fontes
Ham-en-Artois
Bourecq
Mt. Bernenchon
Gonnehem
Robecq
Calonne-sur-la-Lys
Ecquedecques
Burbure
Allouagne
Lozinghem
Ferfay
Auchy-au-Bois
Lillers
Guarbecque
Berguette
Molinghem
Quernes
Witternesse
Lambres
Mametz
Ergny
Hervelinghen
Enguinegatte
Erny-St. Julien
Fontaine-lez-Hermans
Lisbourg
Verchin
Heuchin

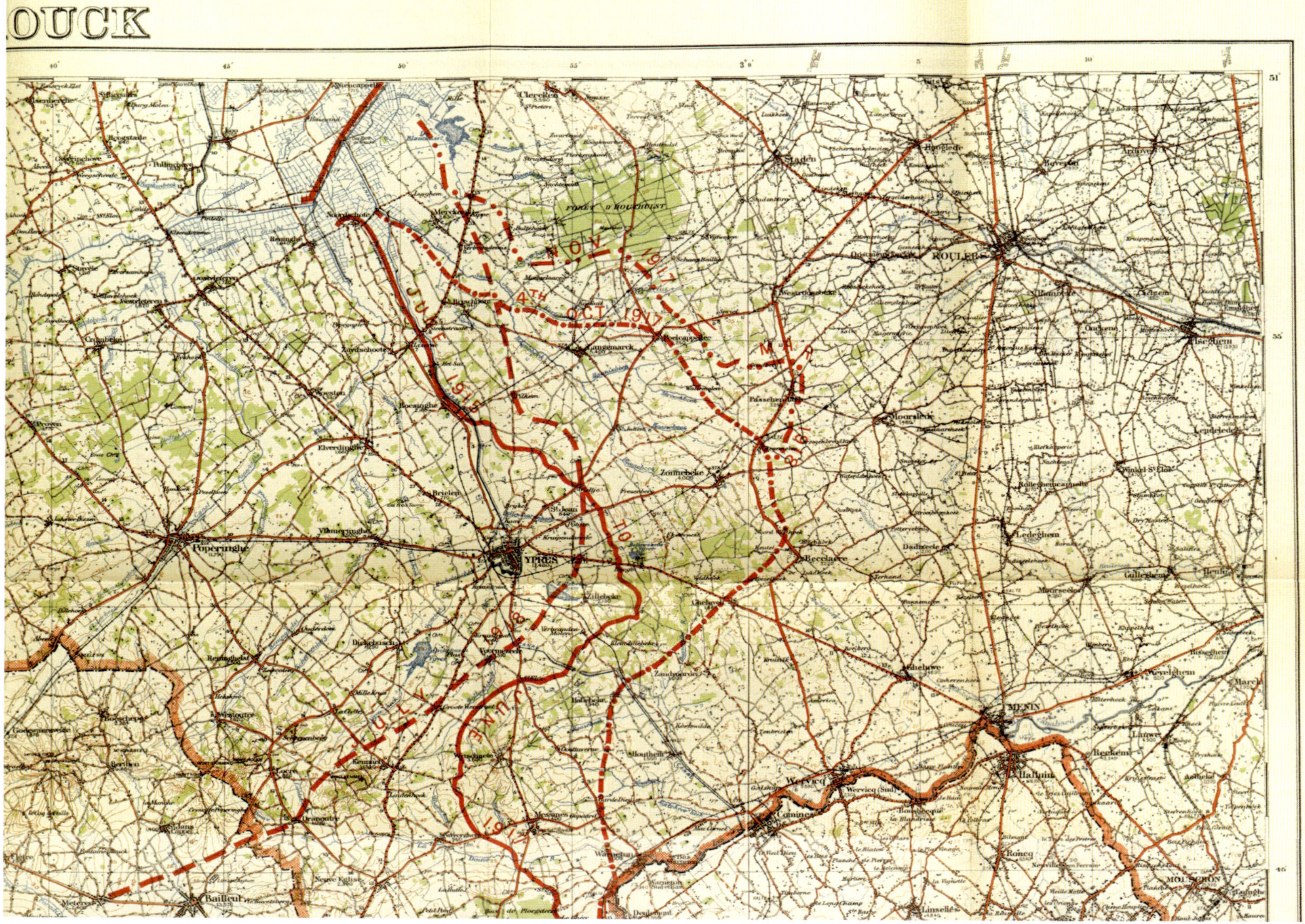
OUCK
YPRES
ROULERS
Poperinghe
MENIN
Halluin
Comines
Wervicq
Bailleul
Langemarck
Passchendaele
Zonnebeke
Moorslede
Ledeghem
Becelaere
Dadizeele
Iseghem
Hooglede
Staden
Messines
Elverdinghe
Vlamertinghe
Zillebeke
Linselles
MOUSCRON
FORET D'HOUTHULST
NOV 1917
4TH OCT 1917
MAR 1918
JUNE 1915
JUNE 1917
JULY 1918
TO

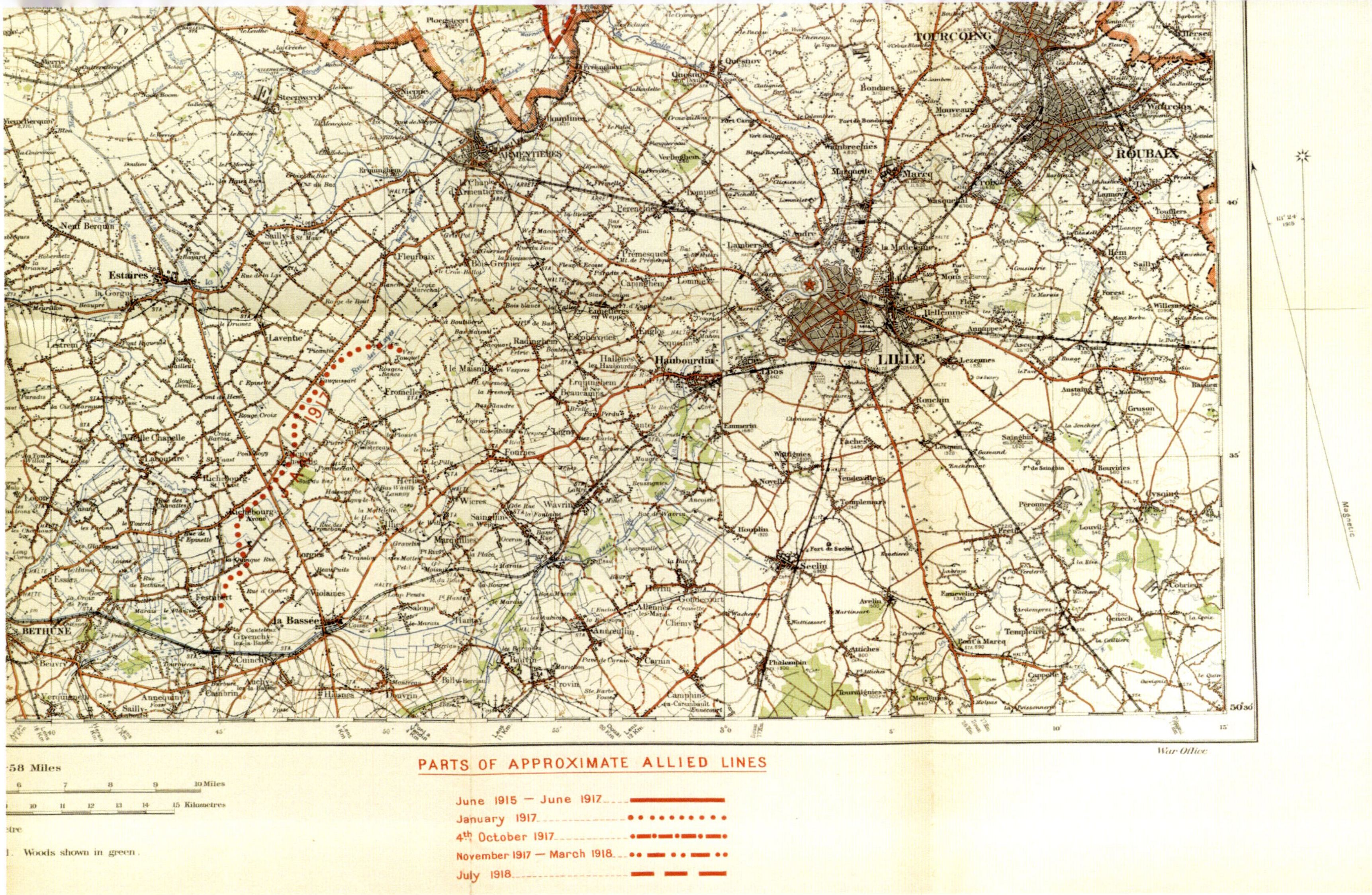
TOURCOING
ROUBAIX
LILLE
ARMENTIERES
Estaires
la Bassée
BETHUNE
Hazebrouck
Seclin
Haubourdin
Neuf Berquin
Steenwerck
Laventie
Fleurbaix
Fournes
Wavrin
Richebourg
Festubert
Magnetic
War Office
·58 Miles
10 Miles
15 Kilometres
1. Woods shown in green.
PARTS OF APPROXIMATE ALLIED LINES
June 1915 — June 1917
January 1917
4th October 1917
November 1917 — March 1918
July 1918
1917

2

FRANCE 1:100,000

LENS

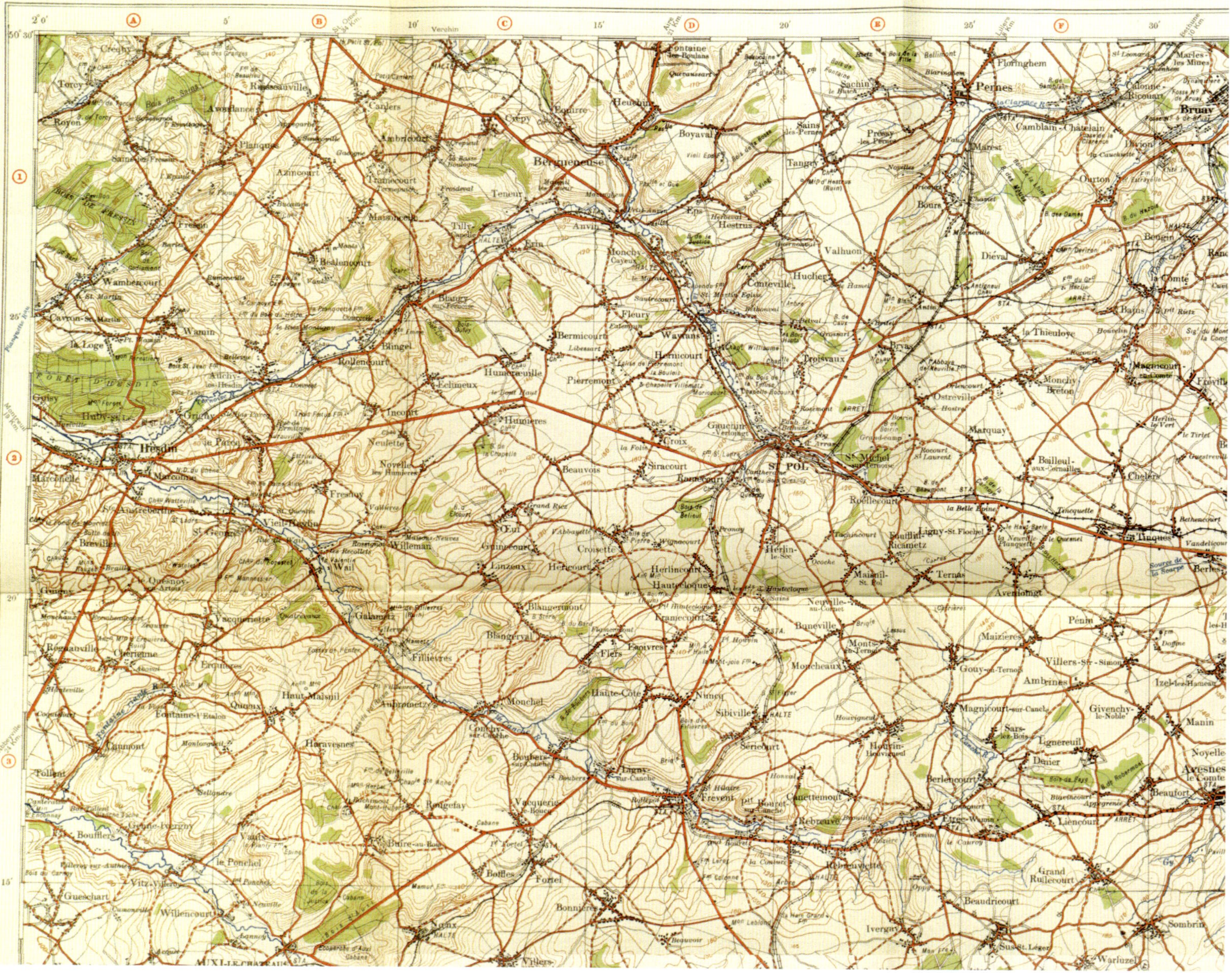

Geographical Section General Staff. No. 2364.

The position of a point may be described on this map by the system used on squared trench maps: *i.e.*, by imagining the sides of the rectangles on the map divided into ten parts, and locating the point by measuring so many parts East and so many North of the S.W. corner of the rectangle. The rectangle is defined by the numbers and letters which appear on the margin. The full reference for a point is thus.

Example:— Bapaume LENS 5K 22

The use of a four figure reference defines a point with greater accuracy.

Example:— Vimy Sta. LENS 2J 86 51

NOTE.—Marginal *number* always to come first; marginal *letter* second; then coordinates *along* and *up*. Never define a point by 3 figures but always by two or four.

REFERENCE

Townships	Thuin
Hamlets	*Lorroir*
Canal or waterway	*Lock, Ferry, Ford, Dam or Weir*
Chateau, Farm	Chau Fe
Church or Chapel, Tower	
Fort	
Frontier line	
Heights in metres (10 metres 32.8 feet)	140
Lighthouse	L.H

Scale 1/100,000 or 1 Inch to 1·5

Mile 1 0 1 2 3 4 5

Kilometre 1 0 1 2 3 4 5 6 7 8 9

1 Centimetre to 1 Kilometr

Contour interval 10 metres, every 100 accentuated.

The system of contouring on this sheet can only be cons

2ND EDITION

11

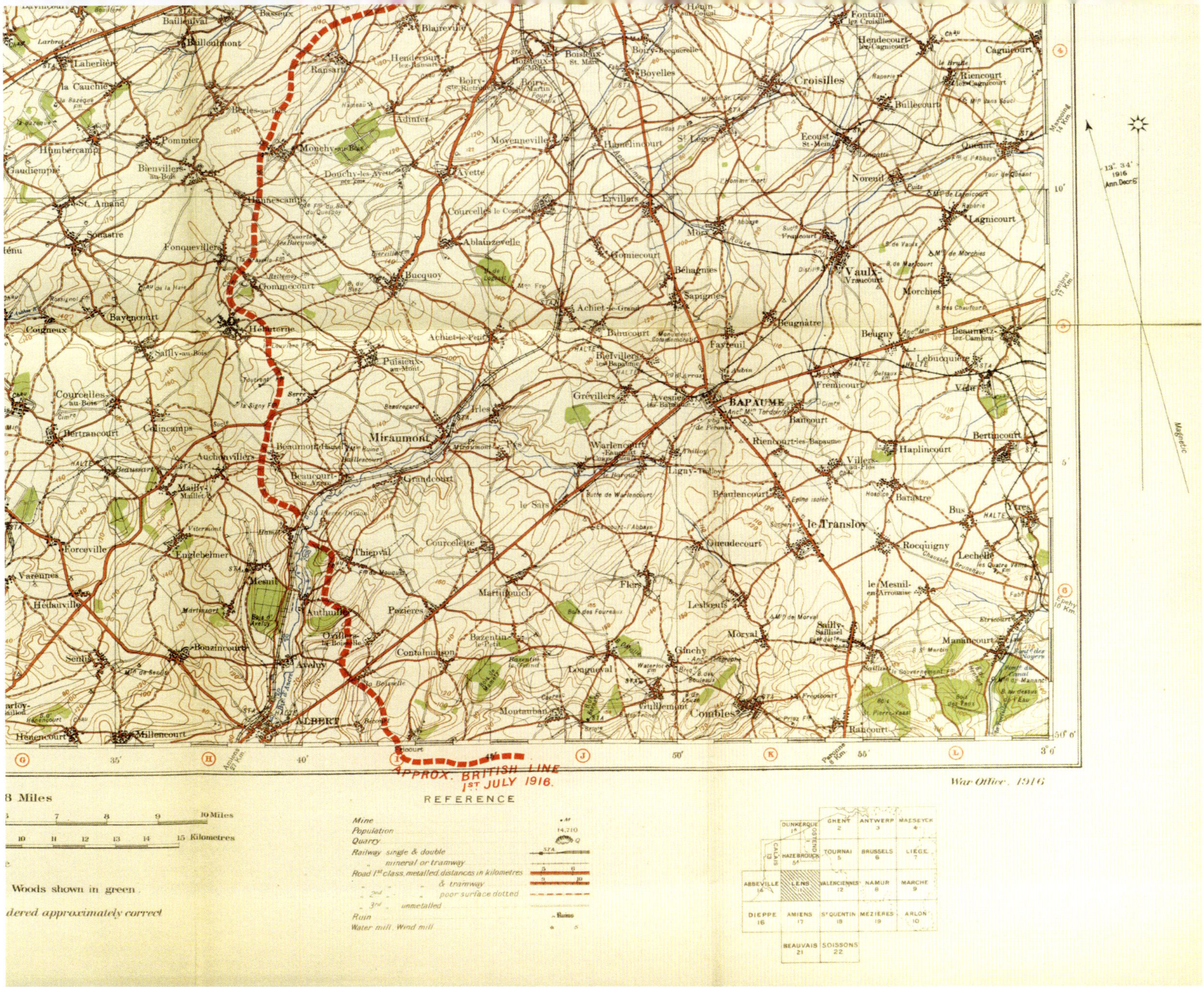
Magnetic
13° 34' 1916 Ann. Dec. 6'
APPROX. BRITISH LINE 1ST JULY 1916.
REFERENCE
Mine
Population
Quarry
Railway single & double
mineral or tramway
Road 1st class metalled distances in kilometres
& tramway
2nd poor surface dotted
3rd unmetalled
Ruin
Water mill Wind mill
Woods shown in green.
dered approximately correct
8 Miles
10 Miles
15 Kilometres
War Office. 1916
DUNKERQUE 1A
OSTEND
GHENT 2
ANTWERP 3
MAESEYCK 4
CALAIS
HAZEBROUCK 5A
TOURNAI 5
BRUSSELS 6
LIEGE 7
ABBEVILLE 14
LENS
VALENCIENNES 12
NAMUR 8
MARCHE 9
DIEPPE 16
AMIENS 17
ST QUENTIN 18
MEZIERES 19
ARLON 10
BEAUVAIS 21
SOISSONS 22
BAPAUME
ALBERT
Miraumont
Croisilles
Vaulx-Vraucourt
le Transloy
Combles
Bucquoy
Thiepval
Pozières
Contalmaison
Longueval
Ginchy
Flers
Martinpuich
Courcelette
Grandcourt
Beaumont-Hamel
Auchonvillers
Mailly-Maillet
Hébuterne
Gommecourt
Hannescamps
Ayette
Ervillers
Achiet-le-Grand
Achiet-le-Petit
Bihucourt
Béhagnies
Sapignies
Beugnâtre
Beugny
Frémicourt
Haplincourt
Bertincourt
Ytres
Lechelle
Rocquigny
Morval
Lesbœufs
Gueudecourt
Warlencourt
Le Sars
Irles
Pys
Grévillers
Biefvillers-lès-Bapaume
Avesnes-lès-Bapaume
Favreuil
Mory
Gomiecourt
Ablainzevelle
Courcelles le Comte
Moyenneville
Hamelincourt
St. Léger
Ecoust-St. Mein
Noreuil
Lagnicourt
Morchies
Beaumetz-lès-Cambrai
Lebucquière
Vélu
Riencourt-lès-Bapaume
Villers-au-Flos
Barastre
Bus
Sailly-Saillisel
le Mesnil-en-Arrouaise
Manancourt
Rancourt
Guillemont
Montauban
Bazentin
Mametz
Fricourt
La Boisselle
Ovillers
Authuille
Aveluy
Mesnil
Englebelmer
Martinsart
Bouzincourt
Senlis
Millencourt
Hénencourt
Hédauville
Varennes
Forceville
Bertrancourt
Colincamps
Courcelles-au-Bois
Sailly-au-Bois
Bayencourt
Fonquevillers
Souastre
St. Amand
Bienvillers-au-Bois
Pommier
Humbercamp
Gaudiempré
Laherlière
la Cauchie
Bailleulmont
Bailleulval
Basseux
Berles-au-Bois
Monchy-au-Bois
Adinfer
Ransart
Blairville
Hendecourt-lès-Ransart
Boiry-Ste. Rictrude
Boiry-St. Martin
Boisleux-St. Marc
Boisleux-au-Mont
Boyelles
Boiry-Becquerelle
Hénin-sur-Cojeul
Fontaine-lès-Croisilles
Hendecourt-lès-Cagnicourt
Cagnicourt
Riencourt-lès-Cagnicourt
Bullecourt
Quéant
Douchy-lès-Ayette
Puisieux-au-Mont
Beaucourt-sur-Ancre
Ligny-Thilloy
Beaulencourt
Bancourt
Thilloy
Le Bosquet

BELGIUM 1:100,000

DUNK

Geographical Section, General Staff, No 2364.

The position of a point may be described on this map by the system used on squared trench maps: *i.e.*, by imagining the sides of the rectangles on the map divided into ten parts, and locating the point by measuring so many parts East and so many North of the S.W. corner of the rectangle. The rectangle is defined by the numbers and letters which appear on the margin. The full reference for a point is thus.

Example:— Dixmude, DUNKERQUE 3K, 44

The use of a four figure reference defines a point with greater accuracy.

Example:— Steene, DUNKERQUE 1K, 9643

NOTE.—Marginal *number* always to come first; marginal *letter* second; then coordinates *along* and *up*. Never define a point by 3 figures but always by two or four.

REFERENCE

Townships .... Thun
Hamlets .... *Lorroir*
Canal or waterway .... *Lock, Ferry, Ford, Dam or Weir*
Chateau, Farm .... Chau Fm
Church or Chapel, Tower
Fort
Frontier line
Heights in metres (10 metres 32·8 feet) 17
Lighthouse .... L.H.
Fathom lines 10 5 3

Scale $\frac{1}{100,000}$ or

Mile 1 0 1 2 3 4

Kilometre 1 0 1 2 3 4 5 6

1 Centimetre

Contour interval 10 me

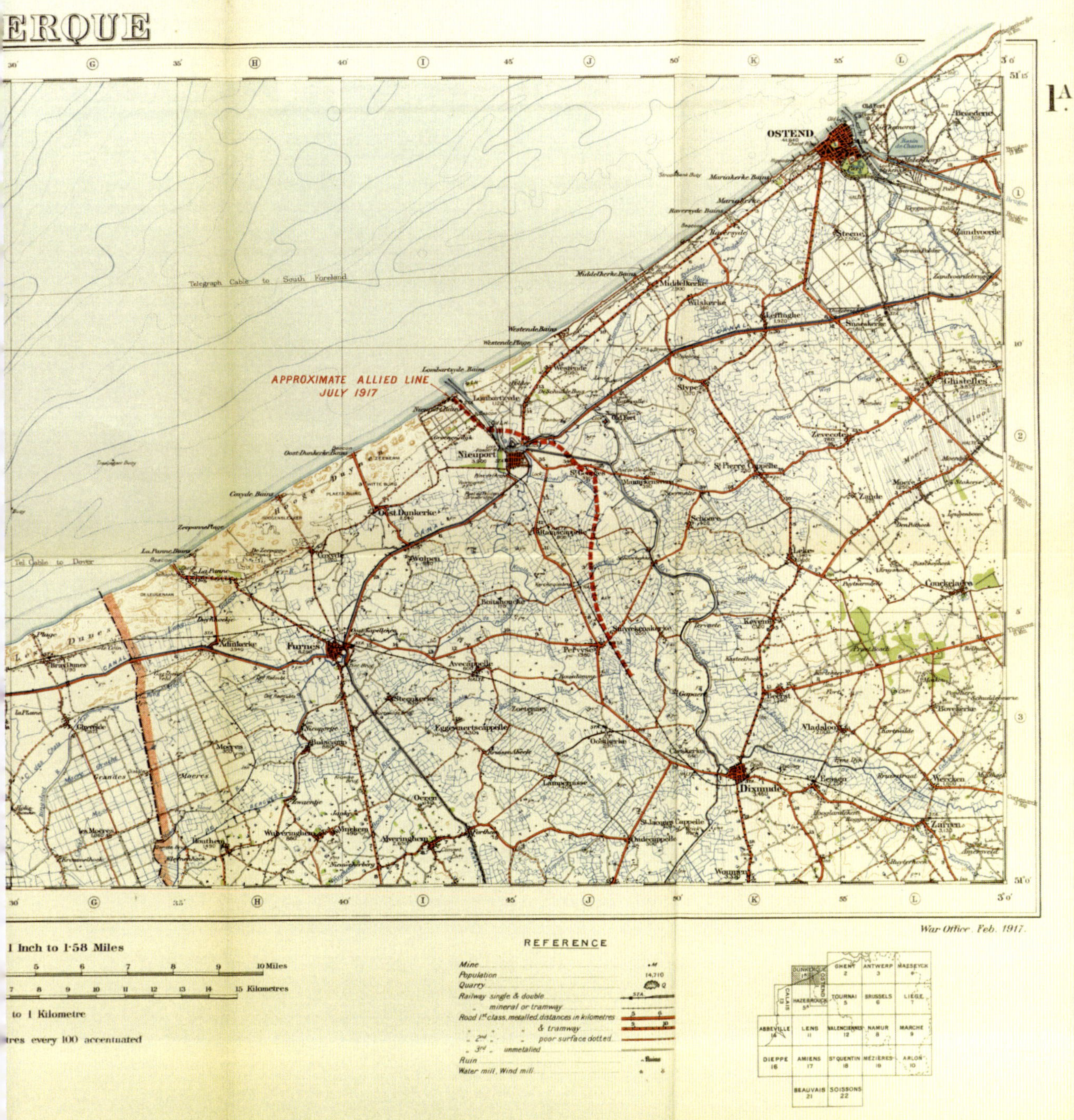

ERQUE
1A
OSTEND
APPROXIMATE ALLIED LINE
JULY 1917
Telegraph Cable to South Foreland
Tel. Cable to Dover
Nieuport
Furnes
Dixmude
Ghistelles
Middelkerke
Leffinghe
Slype
Adinkerke
Coxyde
Oost Dunkerke
Pervyse
Zarren
Woumen
Beerst
Vladsloo
Eessen
Werken
Coucklaere
Zevecote
St Pierre Cappelle
Schoore
Leke
Keyem
Stuyvekenskerke
Ramscappelle
Avecappelle
Steenkerke
Eggewaertscappelle
Zoutenaey
Oostkerke
Caeskerke
Oudecappelle
Lampernisse
Alveringhem
Wulveringhem
Vinckem
Houthem
Booitshoeke
Wulpen
Ghyvelde
Moeres
Steene
Zandvoorde
Snaeskerke
Zande
Moere
War Office, Feb. 1917.
1 Inch to 1·58 Miles
10 Miles
15 Kilometres
to 1 Kilometre
tres every 100 accentuated
REFERENCE
Mine
Population
Quarry
Railway single & double
mineral or tramway
Road 1st class, metalled, distances in kilometres
& tramway
2nd poor surface dotted
3rd unmetalled
Ruin
Water mill, Wind mill
DUNKERQUE 1A
OSTEND
GHENT 2
ANTWERP 3
MAESEYCK 4
CALAIS 13
HAZEBROUCK 5A
TOURNAI 5
BRUSSELS 6
LIEGE 7
ABBEVILLE 14
LENS 11
VALENCIENNES 12
NAMUR 8
MARCHE 9
DIEPPE 16
AMIENS 17
ST QUENTIN 18
MÉZIÈRES 19
ARLON 10
BEAUVAIS 21
SOISSONS 22

BELGIUM 1:100,000

VALENCI

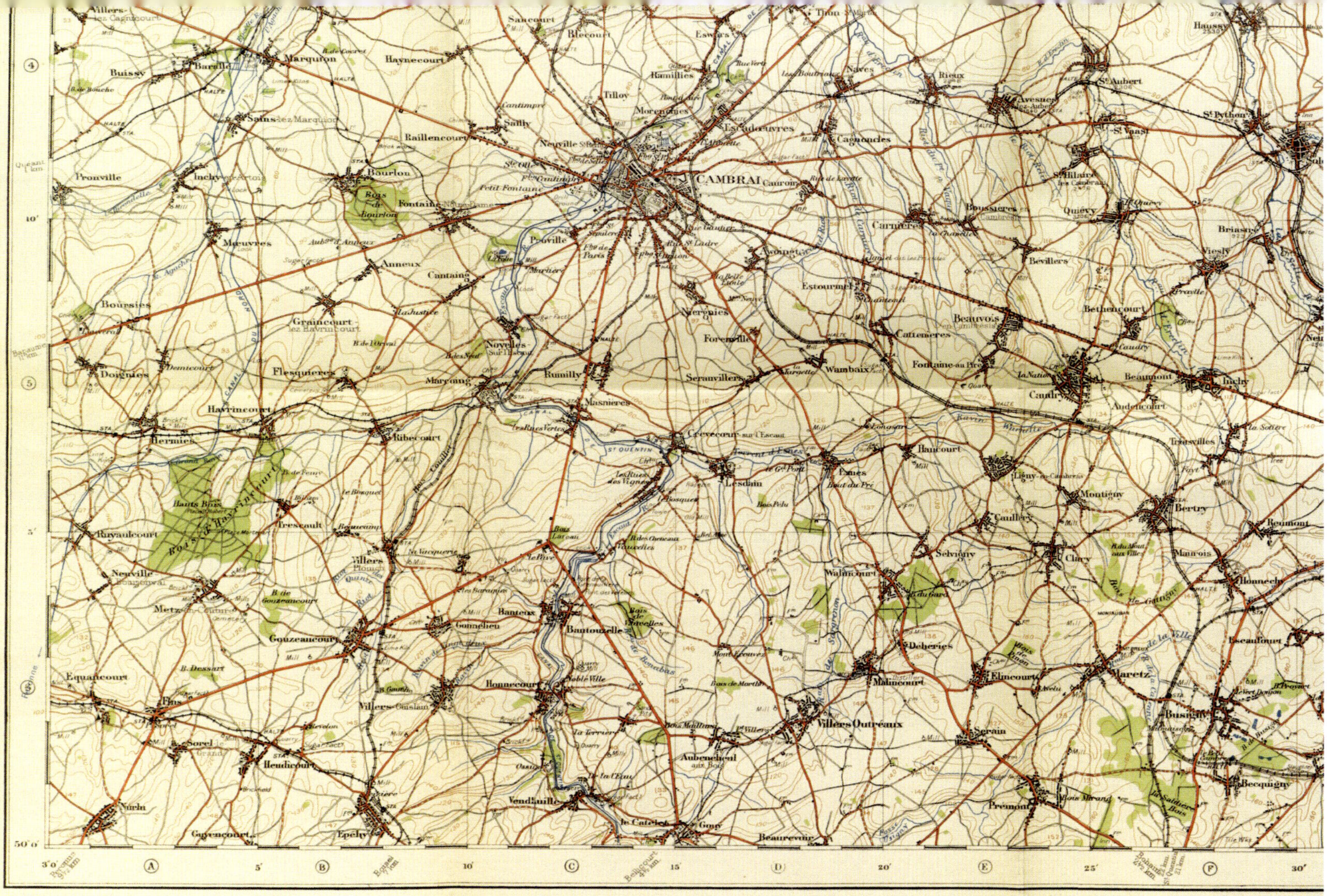

Geographical Section, General Staff, No 2364.

The position of a point may be described on this map by the system used on squared trench maps; *i.e.*, by imagining the sides of the rectangles on the map divided into ten parts, and locating the point by measuring so many parts East and so many North of the S.W. corner of the rectangle. The rectangle is defined by the numbers and letters which appear on the margin. The full reference for a point is thus.

Example:— Favril VALENCIENNES 51 73

The use of a four figure reference defines a point with greater accuracy.

Example:— Amerval VALENCIENNES 5G 50 79

NOTE.—Marginal *number* always to come first; marginal *letter* second; then co-ordinates *along* and *up*. Never define a point by 3 figures but always by two or four.

REFERENCE

Townships	Thuin
Hamlets	*Lorrour*
Canal or waterway	Lock, Ferry, Ford, Dam or Weir
Chateau, Farm	Ch^au^ F^e^
Church or Chapel, Tower	
Fort	
Frontier line	
Heights in metres (10 metres 32.8 feet)	147
Lighthouse	L.H.

Scale $\frac{1}{100,000}$ or 1 In

Mile 1 0 1 2 3 4

Kilometre 1 0 1 2 3 4 5 6 7

1 Centimetre to 1

Contour interval 10 metres

The system of contouring on this sheet can on

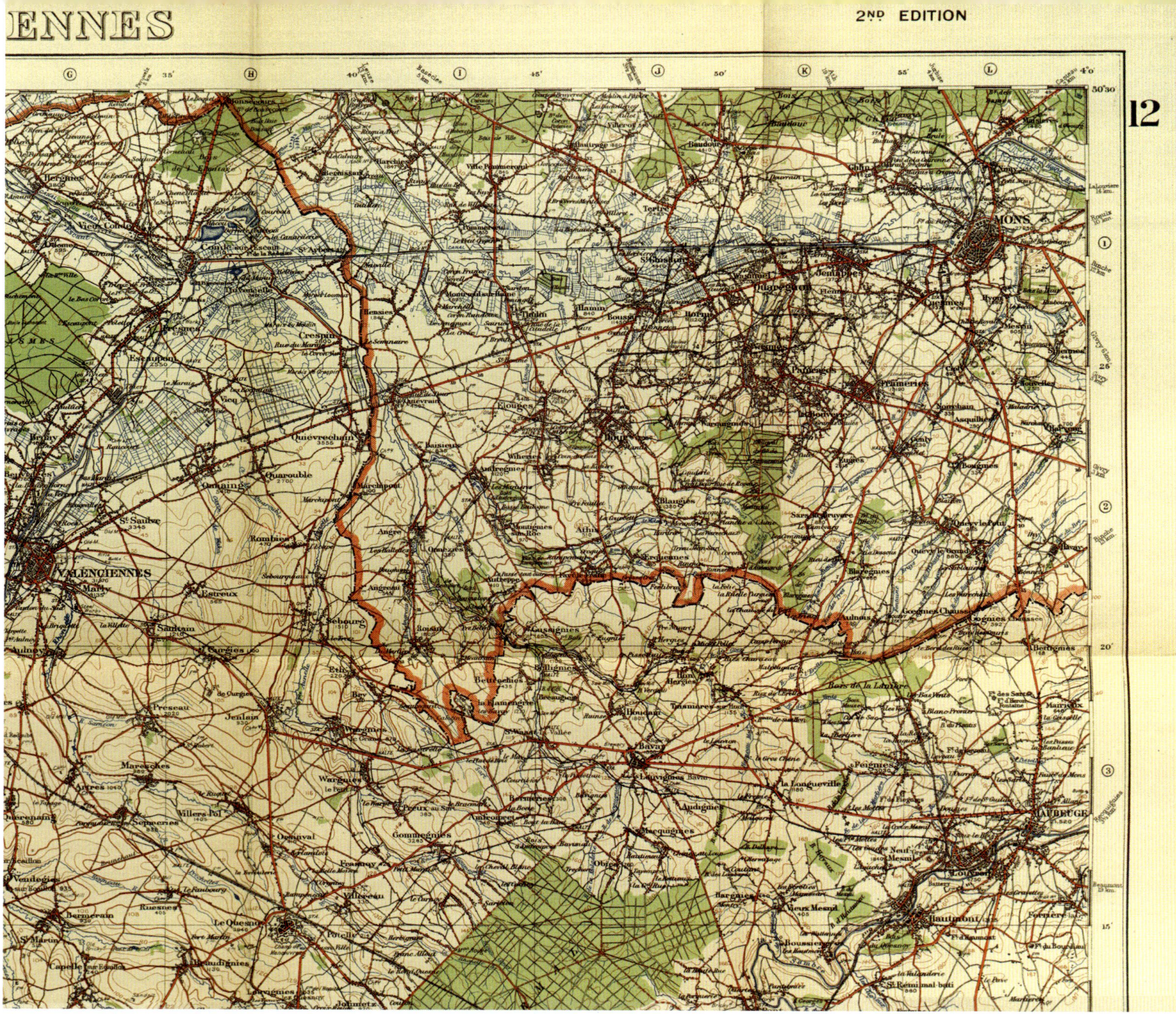
ENNES
2ND EDITION
12
MONS
VALENCIENNES
MAUBEUGE
Bavay
Quievrechain
Quarouble
St. Saulve
Le Quesnoy
Hautmont
Jemappes
Boussu
Frameries
Sebourg
Estreux
Onnaing
Maresches
Villers Pol
Preseau
Jenlain
Wargnies
Gommegnies
Feignies
La Longueville
Louvroil

War Office. April. 1916
REFERENCE
Mine
Population
Quarry
Railway single & double
mineral or tramway
Road 1st class, metalled, distances in kilometres
& tramway
2nd
3rd unmetalled
Ruin
Water mill, Wind mill
ch to 1·58 Miles
10 Miles
15 Kilometres
1 Kilometre
every 100 accentuated
ly be considered approximately correct
Magnetic
13° 19'
1915
Mean Var.
Le Cateau
Landrecies
AVESNES
Prisches
Cartignies
Catillon
Le Nouvion
Berlaimont
Maroilles
Wassigny
Bazuel
Etreux
Boué
Oisy
La Groise
Favril
Marbaix
Avesnelles
Dompierre
Taisnières
Beaurepaire
Floyon
Etrœungt
Boulogne
F O R E T   D E   M O R M A L
Bois l'Evêque
la Queue de Boue
F O R E T   D U   N O U V I O N
DUNKERQUE 1
OSTEND
GHENT 2
ANTWERP 3
MAESEYCK 4
CALAIS 13
HAZEBROUCK 5A
TOURNAI 5
BRUSSELS 6
LIEGE 7
ABBEVILLE 14
LENS 11
VALENCIENNES 12
NAMUR 8
MARCHE 9
DIEPPE 16
AMIENS 17
ST QUENTIN 18
MÉZIÈRES 19
ARLON 10
ROUEN 20
BEAUVAIS 21
SOISSONS 22
REIMS 23

CHAPTER I

AN officer with " Hallamshire " emblazoned on his shoulders sat in a London theatre. Suddenly he became aware of the fact that he was the subject of a hoarsely-whispered conversation behind him.

" Where's Hallamshire? "

" Couldn't say—Scotland, I should think."

" Perhaps he's a Canadian . . .

This, as has been stated, was in London. Though the task of the Hallamshires and of the Division to which they belonged was more often to "stand and wait" in the trenches than to engage in the more widely-known and spectacular attacks of the war, they venture to think that the above question and its answers would have been unnecessary in the Ypres Salient.

Probably no more searching tests of character could be devised than the task of " holding on," and the ability to swallow the disappointment of an indifferent chance and transfer enthusiasm to the next. Long before the end of the war the Hallamshires came to regard themselves as specialists in those tests.

* * * * * *

If the Battalion considered itself unlucky in the shows allotted to it, it had no misgivings concerning the commanding officers under whom it fought.

Lieutenant-Colonel F. Revell-Sutton had been connected with the Battalion since 1899, and had seen service with the Hallamshire contingent in the Boer War, during which he was severely wounded. In 1915 he was invalided home, to the general regret of all ranks, before his Battalion had had time to prove itself, yet it must not be forgotten that he piloted it through the very strenuous and responsible time of training in England.

On the 3rd August, 1915, Major L. J. Wyatt, of the 2nd Battalion North Staffordshire Regiment, arrived to take over command. Major Wyatt (later Brigadier-General) came to the Battalion with twenty-four years of Regular Army experience, including service in South Africa, in Egypt, and in France since September, 1914. During the extraordinarily trying months at Ypres in 1915 the Battalion quickly learned to place its whole trust and confidence in him—

and that not for his experience alone. To officers and men alike he was ever a soldier of the finest type. He was several times mentioned in despatches, and in June, 1916, was awarded the D.S.O. for his services with the Hallamshires.

The departure of Colonel Wyatt, to take up the important duties of Second-in-Command to General Kentish at the Commanding Officers' School at Aldershot in April, 1917, was an immense loss to the Battalion, which, however, was made good to an extraordinary degree by the appointment of Major D. S. Branson to the command. This officer was a Second Lieutenant in charge of the Machine Gun Section at the outbreak of war. He succeeded Captain Williams as Adjutant in October, 1915, and Major E. W. Wilkinson as Second-in-Command in August, 1916. No doubt he gained much valuable training under Colonel Wyatt, but the facts that he was only twenty-three years of age at the time of his appointment to the command; that he commanded the Battalion at the front for two very strenuous years; that he was five times mentioned in despatches, awarded the Military Cross and the D.S.O. with two bars; and that he was placed in charge of the Brigade on two occasions, speak adequately for themselves. In him were combined the energy of a young man and the sagacity and coolness of one twice his age.

Finally, during the period when wounds forced Colonel Branson to be absent, the Battalion was very fortunate in having Ronald Wilson and Gerald Unsworth to take his place. The former's bravery and ability had gained him an M.C. and bar, and he brought the Hallamshires through the anxious times of April-June, 1918, with great credit. Unsworth (of the Royal Warwickshire Regiment) had given up a staff appointment in December, 1917, because he had felt that the only proper place for an infantryman was with a battalion. He took over the duties of C.O. for a day or two in April, 1918 (until Wilson could be fetched back from an Army School), and again from November 2nd, 1918, until the end of the year.

* * * * * *

"The first source from which the regular forces could be recruited was the Territorials. They had been formed before the war on the idea that they were required merely for home defence . . . . . the Territorials volunteered almost in mass for foreign service, and the difficulty was to impress Lord Kitchener with the value of a force with which his absence in the East had made him unfamiliar."(1)

(1) Professor A. F. Pollard: "A Short History of the Great War."

MOBILISATION

1914. AUGUST.

It was fortunate that the outbreak of war found the units of the Territorial Force just at the end of their annual training, and not yet dispersed. The business of mobilisation was therefore very much simpler than it would otherwise have been.

By August 11th, 1914, the Hallamshires found themselves at Doncaster on a war footing under Lieutenant-Colonel B. A. Firth, and in those exciting days quite prepared for immediate orders to proceed overseas. They had, however, many months of service in this country before them, and though the delay was irksome, and the training, in the light of subsequent war experience, inappropriate, nevertheless during those months the Battalion settled down into itself, the officers learnt to know their men, and the men their officers, in a way which had never been possible in the ordinary course of peace training.

Shortly after mobilisation Lieutenant-Colonel B. A. Firth, who had important duties to perform in connection with armaments, resigned, and the command devolved upon Major F. Revell-Sutton.

The ordinary routine training at Doncaster and at Sandbeck Park, where the Battalion moved early in September, was varied by the provision of guards to certain important main line railway bridges and to Vickers' Works in Sheffield, but these duties were turned over to other units when, in the first week of October, it moved to the range at Totley to carry out its musketry course. The stay at Totley was memorable mainly for the atrocious weather, which not only rendered good shooting almost impossible, but also made the camp itself practically uninhabitable; so bad indeed were the conditions that it was necessary to allow numbers of men to go home to Sheffield to sleep, and it spoke well for their keenness that there were very few absentees or defaulters. On November 2nd the Battalion moved to Gainsborough. On the march through Sheffield from Totley the Battalion was halted at the Town Hall, and a few words of farewell were addressed to it by Colonel G. E. Branson, V.D., the Lord Mayor, and late Officer Commanding.

At Gainsborough somewhat tenser conditions prevailed than the Battalion had up to that time experienced. It has since been stated that the authorities were then seriously apprehensive of an enemy raid even if nothing more ambitious were attempted, and orders were received as the Battalion detrained at Gainsborough that it was to be ready to move to the coast at an hour's notice. The frequent recurrence of similar orders perhaps took the edge off our appetites, but there is

1914. DECEMBER.

no doubt that as an immediate result the somewhat monotonous routine of training at Gainsborough was tackled with an added zest.

At length, on the 18th December, we received instructions to relieve the 5th K.O.Y.L.I. on the coast, and the Hallamshires took over a front of some eight miles from a point about two miles north of Mablethorpe to about two miles south of Sutton-on-Sea. It was no doubt highly desirable from the point of view of morale that troops should be known to be stationed on the East Coast, but in the light of subsequent experience it would seem that the authorities were either extremely confident that no attack was to be expected on the Lincolnshire coast at any rate, or that they must have formulated a scheme for real defence based on positions some considerable distance in rear of the actual coast line. It is almost impossible to conceive of a terrain less suitable for defence than the country round Sutton and Mablethorpe. The land as a whole lies below, or at best only a few feet above, sea level, and is protected from the sea only by a very narrow belt of sand dunes; it is flat and devoid of cover of any kind. On the other hand, there is nothing but shoal water to a considerable distance from the coast, and a short steep sea gets up on very little provocation which would make landing in shallow draught boats a precarious business in rough weather. Still, such a landing in fair weather under cover of the guns of an escort would not have been impossible in the face of the only defences we were able to construct. These consisted of trenches dug in sand dunes and entanglements erected on the beach below. The latter suffered considerably with every flood, and the havoc played with the trenches during one spring tide, backed by a sharp north-easter, did not make us over-confident of their ability to withstand anything in the nature of a bombardment. The very concussion of heavy shell explosion would in fact have caused considerable shifting of the loose sand on the dunes and the rapid demolition of the trenches. It should also be mentioned that the Battalion was then equipped with two machine guns only, and for artillery support relied upon one battery of 15-pounders which, in the words of one of their officers, were " capable of hitting the sea." However, we were not attacked, and all was well, while ample and strenuous daily occupation was found in repairing the assaults of wind and tide.

Our next move was to York, and by this time it was generally understood that we had not long to wait before our departure overseas. Apart from the customary field training and route marching—one night march in particular will long remain a pleasant reminiscence with all the participants—the bulk of our time in York was occupied with the re-fitting of the Battalion, the weeding out of the unfit, and a general polish up. In those days one was too keen to grumble, but there was certainly good cause for complaint in respect of the rifles which we finally took to France. It was common knowledge that at this time the Kitchener battalions, the most forward of which were not far beyond the incubating stage, had received new short rifles, whereas we had the old long weapon. Moreover, our peace rifles, which had at least been well cared for, had been withdrawn for sighting alterations, and our final issue was an assortment of really miserable weapons, little better than D.P. rifles, the natural inaccuracy of which had been much increased by an adjustment of the sighting for use with the M.K.VII. high velocity ammunition. Our armourer-sergeant had a busy time with them, but even he was powerless to turn the smooth bores again into rifles. It was commonly supposed that the West Riding Division was to follow the Northumbrian Division abroad, but for some reason their re-fitting was delayed, and in the end we set out before them. In our enthusiasm we were delighted with our luck, but little realised how very great it was. We were sent forward from the base to the purlieus of Fleurbaix, where we were nursed by easy stages into a more or less distant familiarity with War, while the Northumbrian Division on our heels was plunged straight from the coast into the Second Battle of Ypres, and was fighting for its life and the safety of the British line before it had even had time to smell the atmosphere of the line or learnt to know, even as we knew, the immeasurable gulf which separated Training and the Real Thing.

We left York for service abroad on April 13th, preceded by the transport and M.G. detachment, which left on the previous day. A pleasant incident connected with our departure was the arrival of our own 2nd-Line Battalion from Strensall to wish us good-bye and good luck. Nothing of moment marked our journey to Folkestone or our crossing to Boulogne, but it was depressing after a thoroughly fatiguing day, which had begun early, to find on debarkation that we had to march a considerable distance up the cobbled and precipitous streets of Boulogne to a camp on the downs near the wireless station. A steady drizzle did not improve our tempers. Blankets were issued; the men were disposed in small tents scattered over a considerable area; and after much trudging and squelching backwards and forwards by the light of a horse lantern which only served to identify a guy rope or a tent peg when it was too late, everyone was more than ready

1915. APRIL.

to turn in. This eventful day's work closed for us at 4 a.m. on the 14th, and we were at it again at 6 a.m., with orders to issue rations and be ready to move off at 9 a.m.

At that time we moved off for Pont de Briques, where we joined up with our transport and machine gunners, who were coming forward from Havre. A long and wearisome train journey landed us by 7 p.m. at Merville, where we detrained and set out for our first position in the War Area, the village of Doulieu—some four miles distant to the north-east, and about two and a quarter miles north of Estaires. The 5th York and Lancaster Regt., and the 4th and 5th K.O.Y.L.I., who with ourselves formed the 3rd West Riding Brigade, were billeted in neighbouring villages.(1)

* * * * * *

The Officers on the strength of the Battalion when it went abroad were as follows :—

C.O.	Lieutenant-Colonel F. Revell-Sutton.
2nd in Command	Major G. Elliott.
M.O.	Major D. Gray Newton.
Adjutant	Captain R. M. Williams.
Quartermaster	Major M. J. Duggan.
Machine Gun Officer	Lieutenant D. S. Branson.
Transport Officer	Lieutenant F. B. Hewson.
Signalling Officer	Lieutenant T. G. Sorby.
A Company	Captain W. R. Ellison.
	Captain F. H. Wilkinson.
	Lieutenant J. F. Wortley.
	2nd Lieutenant W. Tozer.
	2nd Lieutenant H. K. Wilson.
B Company	Captain E. W. Wilkinson.
	Captain A. K. Wilson.
	2nd Lieutenant C. M. Dixon.
	2nd Lieutenant E. K. Head.
	2nd Lieutenant C. M. Hill,
C Company	Captain H. Steel.
	Captain H. G. Barber.
	Lieutenant A. J. Boyd.
	2nd Lieutenant P. A. Branson.
	2nd Lieutenant P. N. Johnson.
D Company	Captain J. L. Marsh.
	Captain E. M. Holmes.
	2nd Lieutenant J. C. Gow.
	2nd Lieutenant W. Steel.
	2nd Lieutenant J. W. Reynolds.
	2nd Lieutenant L. Hobson.

(1) Soon afterwards the 3rd West Riding Infantry Brigade became the 148th Infantry Brigade, and the West Riding Division the 49th Division.

CHAPTER II

THE FIRST ROUND

(See Map 1)

DOULIEU was a pleasant little village—at that time practically untouched by war—and in the glorious weather of that early Spring, with the fruit trees bursting into blossom and the peasants doing business as usual, there was little to remind us of war save the occasional dull sound of a bursting shell down Neuve Chapelle way, the Verey lights at night, and the never-ending distant mutter of the guns at Ypres. The Germans had been in the place for a short time in 1914, but had done little but gut the church " pour le plaisir de la voir brûler," as the locals said.

Our rest in the orchards of Doulieu, however, did not last long, and within a week of our arrival the officers were sent up in two batches to the line in front of Fleurbaix for instruction. Before the end of April the Battalion marched up to Fleurbaix village preparatory to taking over the sector from the Rifle Brigade. Our Brigade front extended from a point south-east of Bois Grenier nearly to La Boutillerie, but the line was not straight, and we therefore had to defend rather more than a mile and a half of trench line.

The only features of importance were two salients, one on the Bois Grenier—Radinghem road and the other on the Fleurbaix—Bas Maisnil road, where the lines were separated by seventy yards or so, and a certain activity was generally to be expected. For the rest, our front was four hundred yards or more from the opposing line; and once in the trenches there was nothing particular to disturb us, as the enemy's artillery on this front was peculiarly inactive.

Naturally, in war as in anything else, it is better to begin in a small way, and the trenches at Fleurbaix seemed to have been designed to give the inexperienced some chance of getting accustomed to the real war atmosphere in easy stages. Nevertheless, there were frequent reminders of unpleasant possibilities. In the first place, the trenches " were bad and not bullet-proof or connected up." When it is added that the " enemy snipers were rather active," and that the country is perfectly flat, very little imagination is required to complete

1915. APRIL.

the picture. The business of a relief under such circumstances was even more exasperating and unpleasant than usual.

The line consisted of a not too strong breastwork, weakened by dug-outs which were built into the bottom of it. There was no parados to any of the trenches, there were no communication trenches, and the nearest support line was a mile or more in rear—even then normally unoccupied. Much lies behind the bare records : "All men not on duty working all night," and " Much work done on parapet and wire." Though there was very little shelling, snipers were keen, and by day it was not safe to show a head over the parapet. Our own loopholes were so obvious that it was no pleasant task to use them. This activity gave our snipers much food for thought. Attempts were made to re-organise our sniping apparatus more effectively, and in June Captain Ellison, with the assistance of his Q.M.S.[1], invented an ingenious rest on which a rifle could be set to fire on German loopholes without the firer being in any way exposed.

Patrolling on both sides was active throughout the stay. On several occasions our patrols managed to locate working parties on the enemy's wire, and more than once enabled the companies to bring fire on them with success. There were a few direct meetings with enemy patrols, shots were exchanged at short range, and once at least the " enemy's patrols were driven in near their wire." In June, too, the Battalion made its first capture, Sergeant-Major Revitt bringing in from No Man's Land a German flag which the enemy had planted there a night or two earlier.

The normal time in the trenches was at first three days, but this was very soon increased to four and then to five days. The Battalion relieved and was relieved by the 5th York and Lancaster Regt. during the whole period, and time in support was spent in billets in Fleurbaix, a village which still contained a few civilians, and which, with the exception of the church and the houses near, had not been badly damaged. During these periods of " rest " the Battalion was made acquainted with the peculiarly liberal interpretation of this term by the authorities. Working parties were supplied for digging in the support lines at night, and for more trench work and road-mending during the day. Apart from this, the time was spent in removing mud from men, clothes and weapons, and in endeavouring to renew the polish by means of route marches, inspections and drill. This at first was frequently felt to be an unnecessary return to soldiering at home,

(1) Now Lieut. and Q.M. H. L. Cole.

1915. April—May.

but the moral effect of utilising periods of " rest " in this way was appreciated to the full later on.

One of the most noteworthy features of Fleurbaix was the somewhat blind adherence to the current fashion, on both sides, of creating a disturbance at "stand-to," for it must have taken very few of these performances to convince anybody that there never was a more unsuitable time for " stunting "! Everybody was prepared for the worst, and frequently the sole aim seemed to be a desire to remind the other side that there was a war on!

Soon after our arrival there came news of the first gas attack,(1) and the British Army burdened itself with the respirator. The first pattern consisted of a very small pad of cotton wool or lint, and was, if we had known it, almost useless. Luckily, no gas was met with in the Fleurbaix sector to disillusion the Hallamshires.

No important operations, however " minor," fell to the lot of the Battalion at Fleurbaix, but on the 9th May a big attack towards Fromelles was made a couple of miles south of the Division's sector. From a distance the Division had its first view of a bombardment, heavy enough for those days, though it is now well known that our own bombardment was hopelessly inadequate, and that as a result the attack was repulsed with heavy loss. It was sad to learn subsequently that the 8th Division, whom we had relieved, had suffered very heavily, and that a large number of the officers who had guided our first steps during our tour of instruction were either killed or missing. The failure of this attack, it may be remembered, was the immediate cause of the Munitions Controversy which agitated England during the summer of 1915. Had the Division to the south of us made good its ground, the 49th was to follow up the success northwards, and we were therefore fully expecting to "go over" in the course of the day.

To be quite frank, we did not much relish the prospect; to advance across four hundred yards of perfectly flat country against an enemy position entirely undamaged by shell-fire and well supplied with machine guns, is a job which battalions more experienced than we were might well regard with disfavour. As things turned out, we stayed where we were, and of course came in for our share of the consequent shelling of the whole area. During the disturbance we had our first officer casualty—2nd Lieutenant Wilfred Steel, a most capable member of D Company, who was killed by shrapnel.

(1) Ypres, 22nd April, 1915.

1915. MAY.

About this time the value of the bomb as a weapon of trench warfare began to be more generally appreciated, and a Brigade Bomb School was started in Fleurbaix, to which each battalion sent one officer and about thirty men. Apart from some very perfunctory advice and instruction from a regular corporal, who was withdrawn the day the school came into being, we were left very much to our own devices. The "jam tin" and "hair brush" varieties of bomb were then still extant, but less primitive types were coming into use, and our chief preoccupation was to discover how to work the light and heavy friction bombs, the G.S. and rifle grenades, and the Mills bomb. This latter, for instance, was sent up to us without a word of instruction, but its mechanism was successfully explained by the Stores Corporal, who, having removed the base plug and the safety pin, released the lever while peering into the cavity! The bomb luckily was undetonated, so the discovery merely cost him rather a bad black eye. A very remarkable weapon, about the size of a small football, to which was attached a length of what turned out to be instantaneous fuze, and which was fired from a papier-maché tube, caused great astonishment to us and to some of the Great Ones who witnessed its first performance. It shot into the air with a terrific report and melted at about a hundred feet into pale pink dust. What it really was we never discovered, but without question it was not a smoke bomb for covering the withdrawal of patrols, as we had been led to suppose.

The bomb school was a decidedly useful establishment, and a large number of officers and men passed through it during our stay at Fleurbaix. We had not, it is true, much chance there of putting our training into practice, but we had plenty later on, and although the original members of the school may be excused a hearty chuckle when they cast their minds back to some of the episodes of the early days, it was not long before we were profoundly thankful for the experience we had gained there. The school was subsequently carried on with great success in the park of Elverdinghe.

On the 23rd May the 4th K.O.Y.L.I. had their first show and succeeded in advancing their lines about a hundred yards nearer to the Hun. The Hallamshires were ordered to move up in support in full daylight, but had very little to do beyond assuring themselves of the fact that it is no pleasant business to meet shrapnel in the open, especially without the moral support of the steel hat.

On the 26th June the Battalion was relieved by the 2nd Lincolns (8th Division), to whom the Battalion had been attached for instruction in April. Rumours of a move had been current for some time — Egypt, Italy, and several other zones had been confidentially whispered as our destination by various batmen and cooks, but a move from Neuf Berquin to Moulenaker on the 30th, and thence to Watou on the 1st July, rapidly dissolved all doubts. The Battalion had served its apprenticeship and was now to take up far more responsible work.

Mention has been made above of the rather elementary nature of our defences at Fleurbaix, but it may truly be said that during our stay we improved them considerably. Chord trenches were constructed across the bases of the two salients, a great deal of work was done on the parapets and the wire, and strong posts were constructed in the rear of the front line. As a matter of fact, the ground lay so low that it was impossible to dig in to more than about thirty inches without coming to standing water, and we were therefore unable to put into practice all we had learned about deep, narrow and traversed trenches. We worked hard and long, however, to strengthen the position, and it was very soon evident that no one could teach a South Yorkshire brigade much about the use of a pick or shovel. But when we had done our best, much remained to be desired, and in view of the shortage of troops in France at the period a determined attack on our defence south of Armentières during the early summer of 1915 might have been fraught with very serious consequences.

The casualties for more than two months at Fleurbaix, in addition to 2nd Lieutenant Wilfred Steel, included Captain H. G. Barber, slightly wounded. Among other ranks thirteen were killed and forty-five wounded. These figures, of course, seem very small in the light of after events, and prove conclusively enough that the period had been indeed little more than an apprenticeship.

CHAPTER III

THE YPRES SALIENT

(See Map 1)

" . . . . . Still the summer (of 1915) except at Ypres and Festubert, in the Artois and the Argonne, was on the Western Front an easy time for the nerves and bodily comfort of the soldier."—Mr. John Buchan in "Nelson's History of the War."

IT was once said that just as the Poilu's highest qualification was "Verdun," so the British Tommy was inexperienced until he had "done time" in the Ypres Salient. The West Riding Division had not long to wait, but had to pay dearly for its qualifying experience.

Professor Magnus, in his "West Riding Territorials and the Great War," speaks of the Division's stay at Ypres as one of "comparative military inactivity." "It is not easy," he says, "to write the history of those days, when the Division was neither 'in rest' nor 'in action.' " This, so far as the campaign as a whole is concerned, may be true enough. Our Battalion had no attack to make, no attack to repel. If the Battalion was inactive, however (few of its members would have so described it), the inactivity was very closely related to that enjoyed by the man in the stocks—for the enemy had all the advantages of ground and artillery, all the mud to sling. Nothing could be more soul-deadening than the resulting helplessness, and perhaps some account of our Battalion at Ypres will provide a much-needed commentary on the "comparative inactivity" of modern warfare. In any case, Ypres was undoubtedly at that time an exceptional spot in the Allied Line, and one of special responsibility.

At Watou on the 3rd July General Sir H. Plumer, K.C.B., Commanding the Second Army, inspected the 148th Brigade, of which the Hallamshires formed a part; and a further inspection by the VIth Corps Commander, who spoke of the fine appearance of the men and said they were well-equipped and clothed, followed two days later. These events were correctly interpreted as meaning a "warm time."

1915. JULY.

We left Watou on July 6th and spent an extremely unpleasant and wet night "sous la belle étoile" just outside Poperinghe, and on the next evening moved to the neighbourhood of Elverdinghe, and thence to positions in support, just behind the Yser Canal.

If the trenches at Fleurbaix were "bad and not bullet-proof or connected up," those at Ypres almost beggar description. The 148th Brigade was at the northernmost end of the British line where the Ypres Salient bent back to the Yser Canal. The British held the line up to the Canal on the eastern side; the French continued it on the western side. Two days before the Brigade's arrival the 4th Division had succeeded in advancing a few hundred yards.

The Boche was still annoyed, and the captured trenches were in a fearful state. British and German dead lay side by side everywhere; the surviving parapet and parados had been badly knocked about; on the canal bank there was no parados, and more than one man fell a victim to snipers posted in or near the houses clustered round the east end of Boesinghe Bridge, from which position they could enfilade the canal bank for nearly half a mile. Mud and water were in every trench; and there was but one indifferent communication trench. In two places the Germans were within a few yards of our line, and in two others mere ditches held as trenches and projecting out towards the flanks, were entirely "in the air."

The 5th Y. and L. took first knock in the line, and we were distributed between Talana, Malakoff, McMahon and Modder Farms, with H.Q. at Saragossa Farm. The guides detailed to escort us to these posts lost their way, and a fair portion of our first night was spent in wandering up and down looking first for the guides and then for the farms, which turned out to be situated at various distances from the line between the Canal and the Ypres-Elverdinghe Road. Daylight confirmed our suspicion that Boesinghe and Fleurbaix were two very different places. Shelling with much larger stuff than we had hitherto encountered was continuous during the day-time on the line or on the country immediately in rear of it. The Boche, as usual, had the high ground—Pilkem Ridge, in fact—and was not slow to make full use of the observation afforded. It soon became evident that there must be no promiscuous strolling about, as the enemy were apparently prepared to let go a salvo even on a party of three men, while farms and roads were well registered. Rifle batteries swept the road from Modder and Talana to the Canal, and were much used at night upon ration parties and reliefs, with considerable success.

1915. JULY.

The experiences of the first few days may be judged from the following bare information culled from a diary. These at any rate did not strike the Hallamshires as days of " comparative military inactivity " . . . . .

> *July 11th.* At 9 p.m. Battalion relieved 5th Y. and L. Regiment in trenches on east side of Canal, as the 5th had suffered heavy casualties from shell-fire.
>
> *July 12th.* Enemy steadily shelling our trenches all day. Trenches in an awful state. Many English and German dead. No work could be done because of shell-fire.
>
> *July 13th.* Much quieter in the morning, a little shelling in the afternoon, but at 7-30 p.m. enemy started heavy artillery fire all along our line, throwing hundreds of gas shells.[1] Our artillery opened fire twenty minutes after the heavy bombardment commenced. At 8-30 p.m. the enemy opened rapid rifle fire on our trenches, to which we replied. There was the slightest breath of wind blowing towards us, but not enough to take away the poisonous fumes. It is not possible to say how many of the enemy left their trenches to begin the attack, but our artillery fire was now very heavy and most effective, and it was impossible for them to advance. At about 11 p.m. the enemy artillery fire ceased, and our own at 11-30 p.m."

Our total casualties in the two days were three officers wounded (Captain Holmes, 2nd Lieutenants P. A. Branson and Hobson) and seventy-two other ranks killed and wounded. Lieutenant Hobson, an excellent subaltern, died of his wounds.

Altogether we had a most unpleasant evening on July 13th, particularly on the left of the line. It was the first time we had experienced anything like a sustained bombardment, and few people will deny that their first experience of high explosives in quantity induces a thoroughly sickening sensation.

Another factor which contributed much to our discomfort was the ranging of our guns. The position was a tangle of sap-heads, and trenches deserted or half held by each side, while from the artillery point of view the situation had never been properly cleared up after the 4th Division attack. As a result, a good number of heavy salvoes from our own guns landed much nearer to us than they should have done, and we had several casualties from our shrapnel, though this was

(1) These, as a matter of fact, though they were extremely unpleasant and caused great discomfort, were nothing but tear shells, and were not deadly.

mainly due to the fact that shells kept hitting the trees on the west side of the Canal. All wires were of course cut early in the proceedings, and touch with headquarters and the artillery could only be maintained by means of runners who had to pass backwards and forwards through a zone to which the enemy artillery paid considerable attention. The only available bridge by which fresh supplies of ammunition and bombs could reach the front line was a good half mile from the left of our position, where such supplies were particularly urgently needed.

It may be reasonably supposed that if we did not enjoy our evening, the Boche enjoyed his still less. He was well plastered with all sizes and types of shells from 15-pounders to 9.2's, apart from the attention bestowed upon him by the French. How we envied the French infantry in those days! Their gunners were apparently not hampered by shell rations, and they allowed no one to take liberties with the men in the trenches; a round or two from a German battery or trench mortar was sufficient to draw a reply from two or three of the "seventy-five" batteries in the neighbourhood of Boesinghe. Their response was immediate, and not confined to two or three rounds. They were equally ready to lend a hand in any little unpleasantness in our lines, and, tucked into our extremely disagreeable little patch of ground on the east of the Canal, we never ceased to thank Providence for the presence of those batteries and the alacrity with which they came to our assistance. The Boesinghe sector was as nasty a piece of front as the British occupied in the summer of 1915, but we have to thank our Allies for making it a great deal less unhealthy than it would have been without their artillery support.

The Brigade continued to hold this sector for two and a half months, battalions out of the line being either in support in the farms with a company or two sometimes at Elverdinghe, or in reserve in the woods near Koppernolle Bridge.

At the time of our arrival, Elverdinghe, though deserted and much knocked about, was still a village. It was said that as long as we refrained from shelling Pilkem Chateau, the enemy would let Elverdinghe Chateau alone; whether this was correct or not, our Chateau was not shelled, and formed an extremely comfortable billet for our headquarters on occasions, and permanently for a number of French artillery officers. It was surrounded by a well-wooded park which various squadrons of cavalry were turning into a strong post, with innumerable deep and solid trenches; this always appeared to us rather a pointless operation, and we often found it in our hearts to suggest that we should take a turn at digging in the park, while the cavalry furnished a working party to the second line in front of Talana, or carried up rations for a night or two.

Brigade Headquarters were at first situated in a cottage near Solferino Farm, but before very long constant shelling in the immediate neighbourhood indicated that the locality was unhealthy, and the General moved his quarters to Les Trois Tours, a country house just off the Ypres Road near Brielen.

At last, in October, the Brigade moved one sector southwards, relieving the 147th Brigade. Here the Battalion was very much pleased to find more elbow room in front of the Canal, which was now about half a mile in rear of the front line. The Battalion first took over the left subsector, with Headquarters at Glimpse Cottage, and after a week there, followed by a very strenuous few days of fatigue work at the Canal, moved to the right subsector, relieving the 5th Y. and L., with Battalion Headquarters at Lancashire Farm.

From the middle of October to the middle of December the Battalion divided its time, when in the line, between the Glimpse Cottage and Lancashire Farm sectors. The outstanding feature of these areas was MUD. On November 2nd at Glimpse Cottage the trenches were in places three feet deep in mud and water, and could only be held by isolated posts. Two days later, although the weather was brighter, "most of the drains were blocked by falls and it was very difficult to get the water away. The Germans pumped much water out of their trenches and so formed a lake in No Man's Land. Several bays became untenable." Again on the 10th November, when the Battalion was in the Lancashire Farm sector, the Hun repeated the performance, and we were forced to let the water through our parapet. The communication trenches first became rivers, then quickly changed into holes of the stickiest mud, and finally fell in and had to be abandoned. Heavy rain on the 12th November caused Halifax Road communication trench to fall in, and made approach to the first line from Battalion Headquarters very difficult by daylight. The repeated sinking of the parapets and parados, together with the activity of snipers, made walking about dangerous. The present of two hundred and fifty suits of oilskins which the Battalion received from Mr. T. K. Wilson, of Sheffield, at this time was very much appreciated.

The wire in front was not of the best, and sometimes there was no wire at all. Large working parties were, of course, engaged in making good this deficiency and in repairing the trenches, but the weather and heavy shelling prevented the work being in any degree permanently effective. It is hardly necessary to waste words on the "dug-outs" which could be built in such a pleasure ground!

When in support for the Glimpse Cottage or Lancashire Farm sectors, the Battalion was stationed on the Canal Bank; when in reserve, at No. 1 Camp.

In his methods of annoying us the Hun used at Ypres a rich variety of weapons. In the first place, his advantage of higher ground gave him opportunities of which he was not slow to avail himself. Notably, he could observe most of what went on in the angle between the line and the Canal, and, most important of all, the bridges were under direct observation. The condition of our trenches was exceedingly favourable to his snipers, who killed (among others) Lieutenants J. W. Reynolds (7th August), C. M. Dixon (30th August), and R. A. Snow (4th December)—all officers whom the Battalion could ill spare.

As has been said,[1] at the most northerly point of the British line, a distance of only a few yards separated the enemy from ourselves; so that it was not unnatural that bombs, rifle grenades and trench mortars should have become of far greater importance than hitherto.

Our trenches suffered much from the enemy's artillery, and on at least two occasions from fifty to a hundred yards of the front line parapet were blown down. Naturally the proximity of the Canal ensured constant attention from enemy guns in any case; while the authorities had not yet learned the danger of overcrowding. Even communication trenches were packed with men, and our casualties, in consequence, frequently heavy.

At the same time, these insults were not endured lying down. There was undoubted evidence of the skill of our snipers, and our trench mortars did some useful work—on September 12th, for instance, knocking six big gaps in the Hun trenches opposite F 31. And in spite of imperfect communications and shortage of ammunition, there was no doubt as to the ultimate effect of our artillery.

On the whole, continuous exposure to heavy fire in the most unpleasant mud and water reduced the stay at Ypres to a dead level of monotony, but there are a few days which call for special mention.

August 8th was a fine, hot day—and comparatively quiet until

---

(1) See p. 21.

1915. JULY—DECEMBER.

6-30 p.m., when French and British artillery started to bombard the enemy's trenches in front of our lines with one hundred and sixty guns to threaten them with attack. We had moved some of our front line wire the night before. This threat was to draw the enemy and his guns from Hooge, where the real attack was to take place at 3 a.m. on the 9th. The bombardment was kept up till 12-45 a.m., from which time our guns fired odd salvoes till 3 a.m. After this all fire ceased, except rifle fire, which was kept going all the night and day to prevent the enemy mending his wire and parapets.

The reply from enemy guns, the bursts of rapid fire and frequent red lights seemed to indicate that the Boche was sufficiently alarmed. If so, it may be presumed that the attack at Hooge was assisted to some small extent.

On September 23rd an interesting experiment was carried out on the Battalion front. One officer and thirty men were sent up to the front line trenches to assist in a bombardment by letting off smoke puffs from shells. The Germans thought it was real gas, lit all their fire-boxes, and opened heavy artillery and rifle fire.

On October 16th there was a heavy bombardment by the enemy from 1 to 5 p.m.—at first on the front line and then on the supporting companies. The enemy did not attempt to leave the trenches opposite the Hallamshires, but the battalion of the Duke of Wellington's Regiment on our left reported that they beat off a strong patrol which attempted to enter their lines. About one hundred yards of our front line parapet was blown down, and our left support company (D) and Battalion Headquarters were badly knocked about—the remains of Lancashire Farm being quickly set on fire. The total casualties in the Battalion were thirteen killed and thirty-five wounded, including Captain J. L. Marsh, a most efficient officer—killed whilst assisting a wounded man; and Captain and Adjutant R. M. Williams (of whose vigour and gallantry it is impossible to speak too highly)—very seriously wounded.

December 19th achieved world-wide notoriety. On that day, as all the world knows, the enemy made a cloud gas attack against the 6th and 49th Divisions, using phosgene on this occasion for the first time. Although the Hallamshires were not actually in the line at the time of the attack, they were naturally closely affected by it. The Battalion was in rest at No. 1 Camp, but at 5-45 a.m. information of the attack and orders to move were received. All companies were away by 6-30, and marched at intervals for some old trenches some

1915. JULY—DECEMBER.

two thousand yards from the front. Before reaching this point, however, fresh orders were received to proceed to the neighbourhood of Hospital Farm, and there await instructions. Here we remained till 5 p.m., when we were ordered to relieve the 4th K.O.Y.L.I. in the front line at Glimpse Cottage. Although the Canal was heavily shelled all the evening, all companies relieved with very few casualties.

Two incidents of that march up to the line stand out clearly. First, the arrival of seventeen-inch shells in the grounds of Elverdinghe Chateau just as the Battalion approached. Fortunately, none of our men were hit. Secondly, the magnificent driving of the ammunition limbers of the Sheffield Artillery, which went past at a gallop at frequent intervals.

With the presence of cylinder gas, the advent of further supplies of gas shells, and cold, wet weather, the following days were scarcely pleasant—but many sorrows were forgotten three days later.

On the 23rd December a party of officers from a battalion of the East Surreys (24th Division) spent the day in the trenches. The Division WAS TO BE RELIEVED. The 14th Division[1] and not the 24th, in fact, took our place, but that mattered little. So long as we were relieved we had little preference as to which division should do it! No news could have been more welcome.

This last relief was complicated by a gas alarm, but the Battalion eventually got away from Elverdinghe in 'buses at about 3 a.m., and arrived at Steenvoorde about dawn on the 29th.

The casualties suffered during the stay were as follows:—

Officers	killed, 4;	wounded, 10.
Other Ranks	killed, 90;	wounded, 391.

At the time of the relief the Battalion was under the command of Colonel Wyatt, with Major E. W. Wilkinson as Second-in-Command and Captain D. S. Branson as Adjutant. The Companies were commanded by Captain H. K. Wilson (A), Captain P. N. Johnson (B), Captain H. G. Barber (C) and Captain T. G. Sorby (D).

* * * * * *

The Division had little to show for its stay at Ypres in the way of positive result,[2] yet it was good to know that the Higher Commands were not slow to show their appreciation of its work.

(1) This Division (consisting of New Army troops) had actually been warned for Egypt.

(2) So far as the Battalion itself was concerned, the only captures were a couple of Boche prisoners—one (of the 238th Regiment) captured on patrol on October 6th; the other a deserter from the 23rd Hanoverian Regiment!

1915. July—December.

Shortly after the relief, Major-General E. M. Perceval, C.B., who had been appointed to the Command of the Division on July 17th, in succession to Major-General Baldock, C.B., C.M.G. (wounded), circulated a letter which spoke of the six months continuous duty "in the worst trenches of the Allied lines," and said that during the whole of this period the Division had unflinchingly sustained an unrelaxing bombardment and the most trying conditions of weather in permanently flooded trenches with unfailing cheerfulness.

Lieutenant-General Sir J. Keir, K.C.B., Commanding the VI. Corps, inspected the Battalion on September 30th, and took occasion to say that the Brigade had done well to hold the hot corner for two and a half months.

Above all, the Battalion valued the interest taken in it by General Plumer, the famous Commander of the Second Army and Colonel of the York and Lancaster Regiment. On several occasions he visited the Battalion during its brief respites from the trenches. That he should thus spare much of his valuable time was in itself a very handsome compliment, but the following words from his speech to the Division on January 25th, 1916, perhaps go further still:—

> "This is a very pleasant ceremony(1) to me, and I hope to you, with which to finish for the time being my connection, and that of the Second Army, with this Division. I have had the pleasure on two occasions lately . . . . . . and on these two occasions I expressed briefly, but I hope distinctly, my appreciation of the way in which the 49th Division has carried out the duties entrusted to it during the last few months. . . . . . I should like to say to you how sorry I am that you are leaving the Second Army. . . . . . I cannot expect you to share my regret. No one, so far as I know, has felt any deep regret at quitting the Ypres Salient. . . . . . We, I can assure you, will follow your doings with the deepest interest . . . . . . and shall always feel a kind of reflected glory when we hear of the gallant deeds which I am quite sure you are going to accomplish both individually and as a unit."

Finally, it is worthy of note that "John Bull" once asked why the 49th Division had been kept in the Ypres Salient for seven months!

By the decorations awarded to the Battalion this appreciation was shown in another way. The list and the deeds for which they were given will supplement the foregoing sketch of the period at Ypres, but it must be remembered that such deeds were merely the pick of those which were conspicuous.

For the work on the night of July 13th the D.C.M. was awarded to Sergeant W. S. Hutchinson, Private J. W. Biggin and Private J.

(1) Presentation of medal ribbons.

1915. JULY—DECEMBER.

Cowlishaw. They held "the flank of an advance trench, which was partially demolished, for twenty-four hours in an isolated position, extricating themselves and the gun (M.G.) after they had been buried, and keeping the gun in action."

Drummer F. Thickett also received the D.C.M. for magnificent work on the 13/14th July and on the 8/9th August. On the first night, "when the new trench was so heavily attacked, Thickett succeeded in wading through the Canal in order to carry a message from the firing line to Headquarters, although the bridges had been broken and the telephone wires had been cut." He did it again on the second night "under heavy shell and rifle fire, and when all mechanical communication had been broken down he crossed the Canal on a single plank, and took the necessary message to its destination."

The same award was made to L/c A. Crapper, who on the 19/20th December " volunteered to go in search of a ration limber, the horses of which had bolted. He found the limber and brought it to the Canal Bank under very heavy shell fire."

For general good work during the first six months in the country the Military Cross was awarded to Captain and Adjutant R. M. Williams; and the Distinguished Conduct Medal to Sergeant A. W. Clarke and L/c F. Leggatt (a stretcher-bearer).

The following were Mentioned in Despatches on the 1st January, 1916:—

Major and Q.M. M. J. Duggan, Captain and Adjutant R. M. Williams, Captains J. L. Marsh and H. G. Barber, Lieutenants W. Tozer, P. N. Johnson and S. Brooke, Sergeant P. Skelton, L/cs J. Barlow and C. Brown, and Private R. Cross. Major E. W. Longden and Q.M.S. M. N. Deakin, employed at Brigade Headquarters, were also mentioned.

CHAPTER IV

A REST

(See Maps 1 and 2)

ON the 30th December we left Steenvoorde, marching to Cassel Station (about seven miles), where we entrained for Calais, arriving at about 5-30 a.m. Thence we marched to a new camp at Beaumaris. The remark, "Whole Battalion accommodated in tents," sounds pleasant enough—but the date was December 31st! To get right away from the sound of guns was good, but to live on the top of a cliff in bell tents in bad weather was considered scarcely ideal at the time. Moreover, our first experience of bombing aeroplanes as part of a "rest" did not tend to increase our appreciation of the place.

The 11th January saw the end of our stay at Calais, and a three days' march, with stops at Zutkerque and Merkeghem, brought us to Herzeele, a pleasant village with good billets. Here we stayed a fortnight, during which time attention was paid to drill and the training of specialists—in particular of bombers and Lewis-gunners.

Here, too, large numbers of our men who had been detached for "detail" jobs—such as assisting the military police, wood-cutting in Nieppe Forest, or mining—were returned to us; and several new drafts arrived. These, however, mainly consisted of very young boys of poor physique, though they certainly had the great merit of being keen.

On the 3rd February we entrained again at Esquelbecq for an unknown destination (the secret had for once been well kept), and after a fifteen-hour journey we found ourselves at a station on the outskirts of Amiens, whence a ten-mile march, followed by a 'bus ride, brought us to Montagne Le Fayel, about fifteen miles west of Amiens. This journey was the one occasion in the whole war when the Battalion was without rations through a breakdown not connected with the enemy.

On entraining at Esquelbecq an envelope containing maps and bearing the mystic words, "SECRET—NOT TO BE OPENED UNTIL ARRIVAL AT DETRAINING POINT," was handed to the Adjutant. Arriving at Amiens and being told that Montagne, which lies some twenty miles west of Amiens, was our destination, he consulted the maps; but the fact that they were of the country east of Amiens did not help the march very much! This may have been a deep-laid plan to deceive the enemy; or it may have been a joke on the part of the Staff—if the latter, it was not appreciated. The discovery of the mistake at 4 a.m. on a winter's morning was not calculated to improve the C.O.'s temper!

Montagne Le Fayel was in a very dilapidated condition, and there appeared to be much less work done on the land than in Flanders. The Battalion stayed there a week, and then moved in four days *via* Picquigny, Molliens au Bois and Bouzincourt to Martinsart, a village which, though within a couple of miles of the Ancre, had so far escaped much damage from shell-fire. The Transport Lines were established at Hédauville.

In this new area the Division relieved the 32nd Division; and the Hallamshires, after three days in Martinsart Village, relieved the 5th Y. and L. in the front line. At this point we were introduced to Thiepval.

The trenches were cut deep into chalk. Most of them were dry, and the enemy's line was out of sight from the greater part of ours. The afternoon of February 17th (the day on which we relieved the 5th Y. and L.) was almost absurdly peaceful. Enemy trench mortars and rifle grenades provided us with a few unpleasant moments, but our casualties were very few, and our artillery retaliation prompt and adequate; though the British ideas of trench-mortaring in that area seemed to us pretty feeble. The absence of sniping was particularly noticeable after Fleurbaix and Ypres.

After a four days' tour we proceeded to Authuille, a village about half a mile behind the front line. It was in a hollow, and was little damaged considering its proximity to the line. Battalion Headquarters were in a house, but most of the men were in cellars or dugouts—some of them in the South Bluff, where, but for the extreme cold, they were comfortable enough. Seven platoons were used as garrison of the permanent defences of the village, the remainder being available for use as required.

There followed three more days in the front trenches, and the Battalion began to feel comfortably settled — when we were unexpectedly relieved by the 7th Battalion West Riding Regiment, and sent back to Bouzincourt in Divisional Reserve. Four days later we moved to Warloy, and soon after to Louvencourt.

The four villages of Louvencourt, Contay, Talmas and Candas

1916. FEBRUARY—MARCH.

call for more than mere mention. At the first-named the billets were good and the village was about the cleanest we had come across in that part of the country. We were sorry not to stay there longer—until we met Contay. In one's mental picture of this village the sun is always shining; while at Talmas we seemed to be having a summer holiday, and the inhabitants were always kind and the cider excellent. And Candas had a swimming-bath, and was for that reason an even better summer resort!

The Munitions Controversy in England had by this time been settled. For the time being the chief result, so far as we were concerned, was a visit on March 7th from the Munitions Investigators. No less than two hundred and fifty of our men saw splendid visions of England "for the duration," but in the end it was decided that only about a dozen were of more value to their country at home than they were in France.

It was at Louvencourt, too, that the Reverend H. F. Elgood became more closely connected with the Hallamshires, and B Company were very fortunate to have him as a member of their Mess. During the ten days here, there was the usual smartening up by means of drill, and the training of specialists began anew.

On March 15th we moved to Contay, taking over billets from the 7th Battalion West Yorks. Regiment and the 4th Brigade R.F.A. The training of specialists continued, but three to four hundred men were daily sent to work on a new railway which was being built from Daours to Contay—work which was active enough, but an exceedingly pleasant change. On the 30th the whole working party,[1] drawn up in line along the road, was inspected by Lord Kitchener.

The Battalion stayed at Contay until April 4th, when it moved to Talmas, and thence on May 22nd to Candas, where railway work was resumed. Two companies were employed daily on the Candas-Acheux railway, while the remaining companies and the specialists continued their training. From Candas we moved to Puchevillers for a few more days of work on the railway, and on June 23rd the Brigade assembled at Toutencourt and Harponville in preparation for the first Battle of the Somme.

Apart from the work done by the Battalion during this period—work which was in itself the best form of recreation—there was a good deal of opportunity for amusement. There was first of all the gramophone craze—which everybody supported to the full, except the Adju-

(1) Including "Whizz-bang," the Battalion's mascot at the time.

tant and the Transport Officer! The Battalion boasted at this time some half-dozen of these instruments, and officers added records according to their tastes. In these tastes there was much variety, which might have led to friction — but for the fact that volunteers were prompted to carry records in their packs, when the question of leaving them behind at a move was mooted.

There were visits, too, for a few of the Battalion to one or two of the larger towns such as Doullens and Amiens (if only for the chance of replenishing mess stores these visits were much appreciated) and occasional opportunities of seeing the splendid shows provided by the "Tykes," the Divisional Concert Party.

In their turn certain junior officers did their best to amuse the Battalion. Following a hint from the C.O. that even infantry officers should be able to ride, every available horse in the transport became a prospective charger, and the cavalcades which set out from Talmas and other villages were a joy to the onlookers.

The concrete tank on the railway at Candas was indeed a boon, for it made an excellent swimming bath. It was even possible to arrange swimming sports, in the course of which the officers defeated the men in a team race. At Candas, too, there were one or two boxing competitions, wherein more enthusiasm than skill was probably shown; but the competitions were none the less enjoyable for all that.

On April 13th, 1916, the Battalion celebrated the completion of its first year of active service abroad. There remained of those who went out with the Battalion only nine officers and four hundred and thirteen other ranks. The total casualties were approximately:

Officers	6 killed or died of wounds;	13 wounded.
Other ranks	120 ,, ,, ,, ;	440 ,,

* * * * * *

The period discussed above was much more than a rest. This fact rapidly became obvious. Apart from the stimulus of a prospective battle, the authorities would naturally have seized the opportunity of increasing efficiency with all the means in their power. In themselves, therefore, the series of competitions held during the period did not cause any astonishment, but were at the same time a very effective and interesting method of preparation. Attention was paid, of course, to every branch of the Battalion's work, but these competitions were held mainly for the benefit of specialists. It is worthy of note, however, that the Battalion took one First and two Third prizes at the Divisional Horse Show on May 17th, and that a Platoon of B Company (commanded by 2nd Lieutenant A. Firth) was adjudged the smartest in the Brigade in the Platoon Drill and Turn-out Competition.

Several innovations at this time were the result of attempts to organise more effectively first, the specialists of Battalions(1), and secondly, co-operation with other units. As far back as February 29th the Battalion complement of Lewis guns had been made up to six, and at the end of March the Scouts had been organised as a separate section under Lieutenant G. N. Sharpe. The Signal Section was enlarged (mainly by the addition of partially trained signallers from drafts), and an effort made to make it familiar again with methods which might be of use in open warfare.(2) Some effort, with as yet rather poor result, was made to improve communication with aeroplanes by means of powerful lamps and ground sheets. At Montagne Le Fayel in February the machine gunners, under Lieutenants Fyffe and Heath, were detached and a Brigade M.G. Company was formed under Captain Rideal, of the 5th Y. and L. Regiment. Trench mortar (Stokes) experts were also detached early in the year to form a Brigade T.M. Battery.

It was at this time that coloured patches at the back of the collar were adopted by the Brigade. Having completed its first year abroad, the Division did not consider that it had anything to learn from the New Army troops which had been arriving in large numbers during the preceding six months. Many of the New Army battalions wore "distinguishing patches" of various coloured cloth on some part of the jacket, in order that different units and brigades might be easily recognised. Great was the indignation when the 49th Division was ordered to conform, but protests were useless, and shortly after every officer and man of the Hallamshires appeared with a scarlet patch (3-ins. x 2-ins.) on the back of his collar. Many will recall the famous story of a conversation between a Hallamshire and a private of the 5th K.O.Y.L.I. (whose patch was yellow)—it will scarcely bear repetition here.

Indication that a big battle was imminent was not lacking. It was significant that Sir Douglas Haig watched the Battalion carry out

(1) Unfortunately to the detriment of musketry, and the neglect of the primary weapon of the Infantry. It was not until after the Battle of the Somme that the pendulum swung back again, and the rifle was restored to its proper place.

(2) During the trench warfare of Fleurbaix and Ypres the telephone had become the sole means of signalling. The realisation, during the Battle of the Somme, that the enemy was able to "tap" all messages sent on a "DIII" not only led to the "fullerphone," but also recalled the possible value of visual signalling in trench warfare.

an attack practice on May 12th. When, further, a new method of training (the product of trench warfare) was introduced and used, it seemed that some fairly definite plans for the Brigade's future had been made. A piece of ground about a mile square near Naours was marked out with tape and flags so as to represent the enemy trenches which were to be attacked by the Division. Over this ground every battalion was frequently exercised so that everyone concerned should get to know the general appearance of the enemy defences, the distance between prominent points, and the type of problem which might be expected in the actual battle.(1) It was almost an open secret that the ground represented the Thiepval area.

Steel helmets had by this time been issued, though they were as yet scarcely popular; and the forerunner of the box respirator was soon added to the load of the signallers—only, it is feared, to be dumped at the earliest possible moment after the battle had begun! It had been designed to allow signalling to be carried on even in a gas attack.

By the end of June the Battalion was tuned to concert pitch. The long period of rest and careful training had done its work. Given a real chance, the Battalion would have gone far without doubt. It was a very bitter disappointment for all ranks that we should only be pushed into the battle fourteen hours after it had started, and then only to hold on to the original front line.

The King's Birthday Honours List — published at the beginning of June, when the Battalion was at Candas—included:

Lieutenant-Colonel L. J. Wyatt	D.S.O.
Captain H. G. Barber	M.C.
Sergeant W. R. Dodd	M.M.
Lance-Corporal H. C. Porter	M.M.

The following were Mentioned in Despatches during the same month: Lieutenant-Colonel L. J. Wyatt, Captain D. S. Branson, Captain P. N. Johnson, R.S.M. W. Sykes, R.Q.M.S. H. L. Cole, C.S.M. W. Hall, C.S.M. G. Imisson and the Reverend H. F. Elgood, C.F.

In June, to the regret of all ranks, General Dawson, who had been with the Brigade since 1912, left us to take over command of the 39th Division. He was succeeded by Lieutenant-Colonel R. L. Adlercron, D.S.O., of the Cameron Highlanders.

(1) Possibly the fault of this system was too much attention to the "expected." In our own case, for instance, our practice attacks were far more concerned with Authuille Wood than with Thiepval Wood.

CHAPTER V

THE FIRST BATTLE OF THE SOMME

July to September, 1916

(See Map 2)

THE vast preparations, expectations, disappointments; the gains and losses, and the ultimate success of the first Battle of the Somme are common history now. In our share of "the greatest battle the world had ever seen," (1) there were all the preparations, all the expectations born of a long-wished-for chance, bitter disappointments, severe losses—yet no tangible gains, and only a withdrawal from the fight on the eve of triumph. Nevertheless, that triumph would not have been possible without the "spade work" of the months of July, August and September.

It may be well to recall here the cause and result of the battle, and these may best be taken from Sir Douglas Haig's Despatch of December 23rd, 1916.(2)

"The object of that offensive was threefold:

(1) To relieve the pressure on Verdun.

(2) To assist our Allies in the other theatres of the war by stopping any further transfer of German troops from the Western front.

(3) To wear down the strength of the forces opposed to us."

Sir Douglas Haig stated at the close of the despatch that all three objects had been achieved, and added: "Any one of these results is in itself sufficient to justify the Somme battle."

On 1st July the attack extended from Maricourt on the right to the Ancre in front of St. Pierre Divion. "To assist this main attack by holding the enemy's reserves and occupying his artillery, the enemy's trenches north of the Ancre, as far as Serre inclusive, were to be assaulted simultaneously; while further north a subsidiary attack was to be made on both sides of the salient at Gommecourt."(2)

(1) The "Times," 30th December, 1916.

(2) As stated in the Preface, this and all other extracts from Sir D. Haig's Despatches are printed with the authority of the Controller of H.M. Stationery Office.

1916. JULY.

At this time the 49th Division formed part of the Xth Corps under Sir T. L. A. Morland, K.C.B. The front allotted to the Corps extended, roughly, from the south edge of Authuille Wood to the Ancre, with Thiepval as the key of the situation. The defences of this village Sir Douglas Haig himself declared to be "as nearly impregnable as nature, art, and the unstinted labour of nearly two years could make them." (1) The fact that Thiepval did not actually fall until 26th September, when the British line ran half round it, is significant, and clearly shows the difficulty of the Xth Corps' task.

The general scheme of the battle, so far as it concerned the Division, was known as early as the 23rd June. The Corps, consisting of the 36th and 32nd Divisions, as well as ourselves, was to attack, with the 32nd Division on the right and the 36th on the left. The 49th Division infantry was to be concentrated in Aveluy Wood, a mile or so behind the front line, ready to assist either of the leading divisions, whose final objective was about three miles behind the German front line.

It had been intended that the battle should begin on the 29th June, but in the afternoon of the 28th it was put off for two days. The Division eventually moved up to its assembly position during the night of the 30th June/1st July.

Each man carried one hundred and twenty rounds of S.A.A., two sandbags, two bombs and three days' rations. Every third man had also a pick or a shovel. The fighting strength of the Battalion was twenty-six officers and seven hundred and sixty other ranks.

As to the elaborate preliminaries of the battle, it will be sufficient to quote further from Sir Douglas Haig's Despatch:

"Defences of the nature described could only be attacked, with any prospect of success, after careful artillery preparation. It was accordingly decided that our bombardment should begin on the 24th June, and a large force of artillery was brought into action for the purpose.

"Artillery bombardments were also carried out daily at different points on the rest of our front, and during the period from the 24th June to 1st July gas was discharged with good effect at more than forty places along our line upon a frontage which in total amounted to over 15 miles. Some 70 raids, too, were undertaken by our infantry between Gommecourt and our extreme left north of Ypres during the

(1) Sir D. Haig's Despatch, 23/12/16.

week preceding the attack, and these kept one well informed as to the enemy's dispositions, besides serving other useful purposes."

* * * * * *

"On July 1st, at 7-30 a.m., after a final hour of exceptionally violent bombardment, our infantry assault was launched."

(a) First Phase. Thiepval Wood.

July 1st itself was the first of the Battalion's long line of disappointments. We had expected a day of chances and real activity; it proved to be a mere straining at the leash until the chance of seizing the enemy by the throat had vanished. From our position in Aveluy Wood, undisturbed by the enemy, we were left to draw what conclusions we could from the noise and the confused stories of the constant stream of wounded which passed by us.

A minute after 7-30 a.m. we heard a tremendous outburst of machine-gun fire above the whole bombardment; and this seemed to continue practically throughout the day. Naturally, therefore, we concluded that things were not going quite "according to plan"—and anxiously awaited our chance.

At about 9-30 a.m. the 146th Brigade crossed the river to support the 36th Division, and we heard afterwards that it had made a very gallant though fruitless attempt to capture Thiepval. The 5th Y. and L. Regiment left about 4-30 p.m., and the 4th and 5th K.O.Y.L.I. soon afterwards, but the Hallamshires were kept back until 8-30 p.m.—some twelve hours later than we had hoped! The Battalion was then ordered to cross the Ancre and report to Headquarters, 107th Brigade for orders.

Though the actual crossing of the Ancre was peaceful enough, there was a distinct feeling that we were too late. Our first orders on crossing the river only seemed to confirm our suspicions. Headquarters, 107th Brigade (36th Division) were at the south-west corner of Thiepval Wood. We were informed that this brigade was holding the German "C" Line (a mile and a half ahead), and the Battalion was ordered to hold the old British front line round the edge of the Wood. A, B and C Companies (Captains Wilson, Johnson and Barber) were posted in the front line, with D (Captain Wortley) in reserve, near Brigade Headquarters, but it was no easy matter to get them there. It was very dark; the trenches had not been previously reconnoitred; there was considerable shelling; tear gas—with which parts of the wood seemed saturated—was irritating in the extreme, in spite of the goggles issued to meet it, and rendered the problem of finding one's way very difficult; and a stream of R.I.R. (36th Division) was passing through Headquarters at Gordon Castle in considerable confusion. The work of the Irishmen in the morning must have been magnificent; but it now appeared that they would be unable to hold on in the "C" line much longer, if indeed they were in it at all.

The C.O. asked to be allowed to send out patrols for more definite information of the situation in front, but the 107th Brigade were positive that the "C" line was held, and refused permission.

The night was one of nervous uncertainty, of orders issued and cancelled. At 1 a.m. the C.O. was ordered to report at Brigade Headquarters, where he was given instructions to withdraw his Battalion into the Wood and to attack Thiepval Village at 4-30 a.m. As it would have been impossible to do this in the time available, the order was cancelled, and the Battalion was instructed to return to Aveluy Wood. This order, again, was cancelled, though too late to prevent the majority of the Battalion Headquarters and all D Company from setting out. The remainder stayed in position in the front line.

On the morning of the 2nd July the old British front line round Thiepval Wood was held by a mixture of various battalions of the R.I.R., oddments of the 146th Brigade, and three companies of the Hallamshires. Of the German lines there only remained in British possession an area about three hundred yards long by one hundred and fifty yards deep—held by remnants of the R.I.R.

At 7 p.m. the C.O. was called to a conference at Brigade Headquarters, where he received instructions for a re-arrangement of dispositions. Battalion Headquarters were to be moved to Spey Side, on the edge of the marsh and close to the front line; the Battalion was to take over the right of the line, including the captured German trenches, with the 5th Y. and L. Regiment on our left and the 147th Brigade on our right; the 148th Brigade had already taken over from the 107th, and during the night the 36th Divisional troops were to be withdrawn.

B Company relieved the R.I.R. in the "A" line about 2 a.m. on the 3rd. C Company were to have gone with them, but owing to very heavy shelling which caused casualties to runners, the order was not received, and A Company was sent instead, crossing the old "No Man's Land" without a casualty and arriving at about 6 a.m.

A and B Companies had by no means a pleasant time. It had been impossible to get up any rations or water during the nights 1/2nd or 2/3rd, and a water party going across to the "A" line about 10 a.m. was scattered by shrapnel. On the 3rd they had to repel two bombing attacks, and at 8-30 p.m. B Company extended their position by taking in about fifty yards of trench further to the left.

In the meantime C and D Companies were subjected to very heavy and almost continuous shelling.

By the evening of the 3rd the Battalion had suffered two hundred and fifty casualties, including Lieutenant W. R. Favell, killed; Lieutenants Merry, Utterton, Poole and Head, wounded.

At 2 a.m. on the 4th the two companies in the "A" Line were relieved by the 4th K.O.Y.L.I., and came back to the old assembly trenches near Gordon Castle. The Wood was heavily shelled throughout the 5th, and in the evening A and B Companies changed places with C and D.

The front line at this time was held lightly, the main strength being one hundred yards in rear in Whitchurch Street. During the night of the 6/7th C and D Companies found fatigue parties for carrying trench-mortar ammunition to the " A " Line, and also smoke bombs, with which a demonstration was to be made at 7 a.m. Meanwhile, at 2-30 a.m. on the 7th, the enemy attacked the battalion holding the "A" Line and gradually drove them back until at about 5-30 a.m. the whole of their position was abandoned.

It was on the 7th that we lost Captain Graham Barber, whose company was then in the assembly trenches near Gordon Castle. His death was a great blow to the Battalion—he was a most efficient company commander and a most gallant officer.

Recommendations for awards are often a fairly accurate indication of the type of work done. The following extracts are taken from recommendations submitted immediately after the first phase of our experience in the Somme Battle.

Captain P. N. Johnson (afterwards awarded the M.C.) showed "especial gallantry and ability." After leading his company to the relief of the R.I.R.'s in the German "A" Line under intense bombardment, the able way in which he organised the two companies under his command enabled him to repel two determined German bombing attacks. He personally reconnoitred the German "B" Line and brought back four Lewis and two Vickers' guns. During the period 1/8th July he showed "exceptional personal gallantry and cheerfulness which did much to maintain the fighting efficiency of his company."

1916. JULY.

2nd Lieutenant R. E. Wilson (M.C.) As Battalion Bombing Officer on the 2nd July, "during an intense bombardment shewed great gallantry and leadership in organising and maintaining the supply of bombs to the two companies in the German "A" Line. He personally led several carrying parties across "No Man's Land." On the afternoon of the 5th July, when the Germans counter-attacked, he volunteered to guide a company of the 4th K.O.Y.L.I. to support the troops holding the "A" Line, and it was owing to his leadership that the company arrived with comparatively small losses."

Captain C. A. Bernard, R.A.M.C. (M.C.), volunteered to conduct under heavy shell fire a party of stretcher bearers several times across "No Man's Land," and brought in from there and the German "A" Line many wounded men. "I cannot speak too highly," said Colonel Wyatt, "of the good work carried out by this officer under most trying conditions."

Corporal Eaton (awarded the M.M.), "while holding an advance post in the "A" Line, drove off two determined bombing attacks, and throughout the operations, 1/8th July, showed great coolness and personal bravery."

Private Morton and Lance-Corporal Brady (stretcher bearers), *Lance - Corporal Bathe* (signaller) and *Lance - Corporal Levesley* (runner) were also awarded M.M.'s for conspicuous devotion to duty.

There was much good work, too, of course, which was not conspicuous, and perhaps the following letter, written some few days later, will complete the process of bringing into focus these first few days of July :—

"Next day (*i.e.,* the 5th) the Battalion which relieved us in the German line were heavily attacked—they had to send a company up in support which did not know the way. Ronald Wilson (the Battalion Bombing Officer), who had been across many times the day before, offered to lead them, and did so very gallantly. Meanwhile, we were holding the old front line and catching it pretty badly from shelling. This continued with slight variations till the night of the 8/9th, when the Battalion was relieved and came back to the Wood a mile back (Aveluy Wood).

"After reading the above, you will see that it amounts to very little, and that is the disappointing part of the business. We went into action seven hundred and fifty strong, and came out three hundred and seventy, and yet we have nothing to show for these very big losses. The great mistake seems to have been the splitting up and frittering away of our Division at the critical time on the afternoon of the 1st, when we might have achieved something if we had been pushed in hard. . . . . Our men have been splendid—no straggling at all, and they stood the gruelling as though they almost liked it, and when you think that we went in full hope of really getting to work in the open, and in the end merely had to sit in a trench and be shelled to blazes, you can see that they had a lot to put up with. As to the officers, they have all done everything that was asked of them. . . . . The weather was at times unpleasant, as we had several tremendous thunderstorms which flooded the trenches, and by the time we came out we had a number of men with trench feet, even though it was the middle of July."

(b) *Forceville.*

On July 8/9th we were relieved by the 4th and 5th Battalions West Riding Regiment—the relief being completed by about 2 a.m. on the 9th. The Battalion then proceeded to "A" Group assembly trenches in Aveluy Wood, where we stayed two days. The trenches were very wet, there was only one dug-out, and (to add to our discomfort) they were very speedily plastered with gas shells.

On the 11th the 4th K.O.Y.L.I. relieved us, and we were sent back to huts in Martinsart Wood. Here the training of bombers was taken in hand at once, a little steady drill was done, and all endeavoured to make themselves look respectable once more.

The huts in Martinsart Wood were very welcome, and it was most interesting to watch a 12-inch howitzer ("Lucky Jim") at work in our midst. At the same time, we thought he might have been a little more considerate about firing during our sleeping hours! Every time he barked all our candles went out, a cloud of dust came down from the roof, and it seemed as if we were being lifted a yard off our wire beds. We only hoped, each time we were disturbed, that he was making up for some of our disappointments—we envied him his chance of a positive blow.

On the 14th we moved back to Forceville, a distance of six miles. The men's feet were in such a state that this was about as much as they could manage. At Forceville again we were in huts. As we had lost nearly half the Lewis gunners and more than half our bombers, the training of substitutes was taken in hand at once. On the 18th and 19th drafts of one hundred and twenty from the 2/5th Yorkshire Regiment, fifty from the 2/6th Northumberland Fusiliers, thirty-six from the 5th Y. and L. Regiment, and four from the 2nd

Y. and L. Regiment were received. The men of the Yorkshire Regiment had mostly about eighteen months' service, appeared to be well trained—and proved it later. The N.F.'s were Derby men of three months' service; some of the 5th Y. and L. men came from the Third Line, and others had been slightly wounded at the beginning of the month. At the same time, men of our own returning from hospital were sent to the 5th Y. and L. and other Regiments in the Division. The reason for this policy was not apparent, and it was unpopular.

(c) The Leipsig Salient.

From Forceville, on July 20th, the Battalion was hastily moved up to relieve the 8th West Yorkshire Regiment in the Leipsig Salient. This salient, an awkward triangular section of German trenches, about two hundred yards each way, was the only piece of ground which the 32nd Division had managed to retain after their attack on the 1st July. The position had many extremely unpleasant possibilities. In addition to the very exposed crater in the middle, the Boche was within a few yards of us at either end and at several other points in the captured area. Naturally enough, the enemy was intent on driving us out, and we fully expected a harassing time.

In point of fact, our holding of the salient was little else than a repetition of the "frittering away" of valuable trained men. This and the apparent impossibility of increasing the captured area, except with the most elaborate preparations, only increased the disappointment of the Battalion. Later events, of course, showed the value of the footing, for the area was increased, and eventually from it the final attack on Thiepval was made.

The relief itself was carried out without much excitement, but with considerable discomfort. The communication trench (Campbell Avenue) connecting the salient with the old British front line was naturally narrow, rough, and somewhat shallow; and to prevent too easy observation by the enemy, it had been covered in with twigs, leaves and grass.

A and B Companies had had a glimpse of German dug-outs in the "A" Line in front of Thiepval Wood; the Leipsig Salient had several very fair specimens—very deep and safe, but horribly dirty and none too healthy.

We were not left long in suspense. Within a few hours of the completion of the relief the enemy made a determined bombing attack on two saps which were held by B Company. He penetrated into the

1916. JULY.

trench, but was driven out at a cost of some thirty-five casualties, including 2nd Lieutenant C. McCarraher, who, standing 6-ft. 5-ins. in his socks, found conditions in the Leipsig Salient distinctly trying.

The situation was one of very great anxiety—the proximity of the enemy meant, on the one hand, absolutely no rest, for anything might happen at a moment's notice; on the other hand, extreme difficulty in preparing any offensive action. Nevertheless, at 8-30 p.m. on the 22nd, the G.O.C. Brigade arrived at Battalion Headquarters and informed the C.O. that an attack must be made during the night in order to secure a rough parallelogram of ground about fifty yards by one hundred and twenty. There was little time to arrange matters, artillery preparations were out of the question from the nature of the position, and it was decided to carry out the attack by bombers only. Zero time was to be 1 a.m.

Our men had several insults to avenge, but from the first all the cards were in the enemy's hands—time, ground, the scarcity of our trained bombers. What bombers we had made their way down the communicating trenches at the end, but found them full of wire, while the enemy bombed them from "T" trenches at the side. It was impossible to get on, and our men had to return to the original line—once more with nothing but casualties to our precious bombers (six killed, thirty-six wounded, one missing) to show for their effort. Sergeant S. E. Warburton was later awarded the Military Medal in recognition of his personal gallantry during this attempt.

At mid-day we were relieved and moved to the S. Bluff, near Authuille, leaving two companies in support of the 4th K.O.Y.L.I., who were now holding the salient. On the 24th we returned for two fairly peaceful days, the chief pastimes being the cleaning of bombs and the scattering of large parties of Germans seen in the open near Mouquet Farm.

These two days in the salient were followed by a week in close support at Wood Post, where we relieved the 5th Y. and L. Regiment. Two companies held the old British front line, one was at Wood Post, and the fourth in reserve near the river. The front line had a fairly quiet time, and many of the men were able to go down to the Ancre for a bathe. Wood Post itself, however, was a most unpleasant spot. It was frequently shelled, the dug-outs afforded no protection (it was here that Lieutenants H. E. Dyson, G. N. Sharpe and P. S. Koe were all killed in their dug-out by a single shell), there were no trenches in which to shelter, and "Lightning Alley," leading away from it, did its best to live up to its name.

The delights of the place were enhanced by our heavy trench mortars, who at this time struck a very poor line in fuses, with the result that everybody, including the T.M. officers themselves, completely lost confidence in the weapons. " I have the misfortune to be," said one to our C.O., very dismally, "the heavy Trench Mortar Officer. I have been ordered to fire. Will you please clear your front line? "

On August 3rd the Brigade, less the Hallamshires, was relieved by the 146th Brigade, but on the following day the 5th K.O.Y.L.I. took our place, and we went back to Martinsart Wood and the twelve-inch howitzer for three days. Nightly working parties were the feature of the stay this time. For two nights most of the Brigade was employed in digging assembly trenches in front of Thiepval Wood. Why the enemy allowed us to carry out our purpose practically unmolested will ever remain a mystery. Despite every effort, the picks and shovels seemed to be making an infernal din as the men moved up to the site for the new trenches, and the nights were not particularly dark. However, working on the supposition that we should be disturbed, and that "right early," our men got on with the job splendidly, although the soil was mainly solid chalk.

After three days in Martinsart Wood the Battalion moved back for a very welcome rest at Hédauville and Puchevillers. There were large working parties, and one more attempt to get the Battalion properly cleaned up and re-organised.

(d) *The Woods Again.*

The 26th August saw us once more in Aveluy Wood, where we relieved the 2nd South Lancashire Regiment (25th Division). The appalling weather and the return to working parties in Thiepval Wood (largely a matter of carrying on the tramway along Spey Side) were not encouraging, and a message from the Commander-in-Chief could not have been better timed. "I do not think that any troops could have fought better than the 49th Division," said Sir Douglas Haig, "and I am proud to have you under my command." A message of that type meant much—for it showed that the dull and expensive drudgery of our Somme experience was not only valuable to the main issue after all, but that the fact was appreciated.

The 146th and 147th Brigades were now preparing for another

1916. SEPTEMBER.

attack, the object of which was to capture the first two lines of trenches between Thiepval Village and the Ancre. The 148th Brigade was to follow through if this attack was successful, and to swing round and attack the village itself from a new direction. The Battalion moved to Martinsart Wood, bombs and extra S.A.A. were issued, hopes again ran high; but once more the attack from Thiepval Wood failed, and once more the Hallamshires were destined to do nothing more glorious than take over the old front line on the night after the attack.

All four companies were in the line and Battalion Headquarters were at Belfast City. The line was not quite the same as it had been at the beginning of July, for we now held the assembly trenches in front of the wood instead of the line round the edge of the wood itself. Otherwise, conditions were not dissimilar, and the 7th September was as bad a day as any that had been endured in July, the enemy treating us to a particularly heavy bombardment, which included much gas and caused over a hundred casualties. Among these were Lieutenants Head[1] and Seagrave, who were both wounded.

After this outburst of hatred matters were fairly quiet until we were relieved by the 4th K.O.Y.L.I. on the 11th, and proceeded to the North Bluff, just east of the river.

Military Medals were later awarded to:

Lance-Corporal Freeman for digging out, in full view of the enemy, two men who had been buried on the 4th September; and to

Privates J. Jelley and *E. Gray* for gallantry when in charge of Lewis guns on the 6th September.

(e) We turn our backs on the Somme.

On the North Bluff parties were daily found for the R.E.—for carrying and digging. Dug-outs here looked serviceable enough, but crumpled in most disconcerting fashion as soon as shells began to arrive. We were lucky in not having more numerous casualties. We received several drafts, and some attempt was made to train reserve specialists.

The few days we spent there, however, would have been quite uneventful but for a raid carried out by a party under 2nd Lieutenant Christmas. The authorities always appeared to think highly of the moral value of this type of raid. This view was amply justified when the raid proved a success, but infantrymen were very dubious as to the general gain because so often a raid meant heavy losses for very small

(1) Lieut. Head died of his wounds three months later.

1914. SEPTEMBER.

results. However, that really was no business of the troops in the line, and, doubtless, on this occasion, an identification of the German units opposite us would have been of the utmost value.

Preparations for the raid included the blackening of the raiders' faces, the removal of all identification marks and papers, and the issue of razors and knobkerries. Lieutenant Christmas took with him twelve picked volunteers, and they were to make for the "Pope's Nose." The story of the raid may perhaps best be told in the words of the official report. It will be seen that, although no identification was obtained, this fact was due to no lack of effort—and having failed thus far, the party did the next best thing, and brought back information which might well have been valuable.

" . . . . . . Lieutenant Christmas took out his Sergeants at about 12-30 a.m. to reconnoitre. He then returned and took out his flanking parties. As soon as these were in position he fetched his raiding party and lay out about fifty yards from the German trench. He himself went a little in advance of his party with Sergeant Shute. On the barrage starting, he found the shells falling near him. . . . . . A Verey light went up in front of him, and he decided to go forward at once. On reaching the front line they found the Verey light had been sent up from the 2nd line. They found no Germans, and turned to the right as previously arranged. . . . . They proceeded about fifty yards without meeting any opposition, when Lieutenant Christmas was wounded and the two men near him were killed by shell fire. Sergeant Shute tried to get to Lieutenant Christmas across the wire, but, finding it too thick at this point, went a little further and brought him down the sap at point 91.

"The trench was found to be very much knocked about, in some places only two feet deep. Two concrete emplacements intact, and two dug-outs which were blown in were entered, but no one was found. Sergeant Shute saw a communicating trench which was in a fairly good state; a block had been put up a little way up the trench. There was practically no wire where the party entered the trench, only a few stakes being left, but further to the right it seemed to be in a fairly good state.

"Verey lights were thrown up from the German Support Line. . . . . . Later, on going out to bring in the wounded, Sergeant Shute reported some enemy trench-mortar fire. Casualties are estimated at, among the raiding party, one officer and eight other ranks; in the flanking party, five other ranks. The strength of the raiding party, was one officer and eleven other ranks, and of the flanking party fourteen other ranks.

"Sergeant Shute, after taking Lieutenant Christmas to the British Line, went back twice to bring in wounded, and appears to have behaved with the greatest gallantry and coolness throughout."

For their work on this occasion Lieutenant Christmas won the M.C., Sergeant G. A. Shute the D.C.M., and Lance-Corporal S. Ibbotson the M.M.

A further attempt was made by a party under Lieutenant Stanley Brooke a few days later, but the German wire was uncut, and the party was forced to return.

During the two following days the Battalion moved to Varennes, and was immensely cheered by the announcement that three nights of hard work would bring in their wake a thorough rest at last. The Battalion had to find from five hundred to five hundred and fifty men on each of these nights for the most unpleasant work in the Leipsig Salient. During August our foothold there had been gradually extended, and it was now determined to make yet another attack on Thiepval, this time from the south. Our task was to dig a "jumping-off" trench, in order that the attacking troops might at least start their movement in the right direction. The whole country was by this time so churned up by shell-fire that no landmarks were visible, and only very short isolated bits of trench could be kept clear—hence the forming up for an attack was no easy matter.

The working parties left camp at 5 p.m. and usually returned about 6 a.m. completely worn out, but such were the difficulties of getting to and from the front line that it is doubtful if more than a couple of hours' work was done. The nights were very dark; there was heavy shelling throughout; it was extremely hard to see how less than weeks of work under peace conditions could restore order out of that chaos; R.E. guides seemed rarely to know the best routes (but who did?), and always to expect miracles from the men—there could be no more soul-destroying experience. But there was that REST . . . . !

Within three days, when Thiepval was about to fall, the Battalion was in the line again, in front of Souastre, north of the Ancre!

* * * * * *

On July 1st, 1916, after its long period out of the line, the Battalion flattered itself that it was as fit and well-trained as any in the country. It felt able to take its share in "the greatest battle the world has ever seen," yet, in point of fact, one small bombing attack was the only offensive operation carried out. For nearly three months life consisted of alternate periods of enduring bombardment in shelterless trenches and of finding working parties of the most strenuous description. The casualties were twenty-one officers and seven hundred and fifty other ranks.

Before leaving the history of our share in the Somme Battle it will be as well to append the list of awards and mentions from the Despatches of January, 1917, because the work, of which these awards were the recognition, was mainly, if not entirely, done during the months of July, August and September, 1916.

Major D. S. Branson was awarded the M.C.; C.S.M. G. Imisson the D.C.M.; while Lieutenant-Colonel L. J. Wyatt, D.S.O., R.S.M. W. Sykes and Lance-Corporal W. Fell (Medical Officer's Orderly) were "mentioned."

In August Major E. W. Wilkinson was transferred to England sick—Captain D. S. Branson took his place as Second in Command, while 2nd Lieutenant D. P. Grant became Adjutant. Lieutenant F. B. Hewson, the Transport Officer, was appointed Staff Captain of the 148th Brigade on August 25th, and, subsequently, became a Brigade Major in the 66th Division. His services on the Staff were later rewarded by a D.S.O. and an M.C.

CHAPTER VI

October to December, 1916

(See Map 2)

WHILE the last stages of the Somme Battle of 1916 were in progress the Hallamshires were destined to *read* of the great progress made, as they sat in trenches just north of the battle area.

September 26th was spent in preparation for the relief of the 16th K.R.R. in the front line at Fonquevillers. In spite of the disappointment at the loss of the promised rest, the men were in excellent spirits. Guides were met near a ruined shrine on the road-side, and each platoon in turn disappeared into the darkness. The very bad condition of the trenches and the darkness of the night made the task of taking over a new sector even more unpleasant and difficult than usual, and the relief was not complete before the early hours of the morning.

From that time until 26th November the Battalion enjoyed the trivial round of trench life at its dullest—wet trenches—shelling—working parties—cleaning up—training. The trenches at Fonquevillers (September 26—October 3), in front of Hébuterne (October 25-31, November 6-12), and in front of Bienvillers (November 18-26) were in a very bad condition as a result of recent rain, and they were held usually by a chain of Lewis-gun or bombing posts, with the remainder of each company in close support. Every effort was made on our part to improve the trenches, and on the part of the Boche (by means of artillery and accurate T.M. fire) to make them worse. Fortunately, the Boche did more damage to our trenches than to our personnel, though at Fonquevillers one T.M. caused several casualties to a Lewis-gun team; and on the 23rd November, while raiding the West Yorks. on our flank, the enemy bombarded our left with minenwerfer. In the latter case six men were knocked out (two killed) and 2nd Lieutenant R. T. Kerr was reported "missing, believed killed."

Most of our time out of the front line was spent either in Hébuterne (in support) or at Souastre (Brigade reserve). Working parties were the feature of both, but the village of Hébuterne was always unhealthy. On October 22nd the enemy attempted a raid on the 4th K.O.Y.L.I. lines, and two of our companies were immediately sent to the "Keep," as it was expected that there would be an attack on a larger scale. The raiders, however, were either killed or driven off, and when the shelling, which had been heavy both in the line and Hébuterne itself, had died down, our two companies returned to their position in the village.

Less unpleasant days were spent at Bienvillers, Sombrin and St. Amand, where some training was carried out. In particular, subalterns, who had recently joined the Battalion, were instructed in the regimental method of guard-mounting, etc., N.C.O.'s classes were formed so that the gaps caused by the Somme Battle could be more efficiently filled, and there were lectures. At St. Amand, a Divisional Rifle Range was completed, and one company fired on it—the first opportunity for practice in shooting the Battalion had had for months. Here, too, the Battalion was fitted with the new small box respirators.

On December 4th the 5th North Staffs. relieved us at St. Amand and we marched to Sus-St. Leger *via* Gaudiempré-Couterelle-Coullement for the rest which had been promised when we left the Somme area at the end of September.

At Sus-St. Leger the Battalion was destined to remain for more than a month, in what were perhaps the best billets we had during the whole war. A better place for a rest could not have been found. The people of the village quite took the men to their hearts, and in many small ways added to their comfort, while there were several estaminets where they could enjoy a glass of good beer and a "sing-song." Excellent fields were available, and several competitions were arranged—including football, as well as others of a more military nature.

On December 7th R.S.M. Sykes left for England (time expired) after nine years' service as R.S.M. of the Hallamshires. He was succeeded by C.S.M. Imisson, who remained with the Battalion as R.S.M. until the end of the war, and who, in the course of the campaign, was awarded the M.C., D.C.M., M.M., and Belgian Croix de Guerre.

The lectures, already mentioned, were a form of torture designed to prevent officers and N.C.O.'s from having too "cushy" a time when out of the line. Some unfortunate subaltern would be ordered to lecture, and the remainder were equally unfortunate in having to listen to him. As often as not the Brigadier was present, and this did not add to the comfort of the lecturer. Captain L. A. Wilkins gave

1916. DECEMBER.

a rather sanguinary lecture on "The Spirit of the Bayonet," Lieut. King told us of the horrors of thirst endured by our men in German South-West Africa, while other subjects were "Musketry," "Discipline," and so forth.

General Allenby visited the Battalion whilst carrying out daily training on December 28th, and the day before General Snow, the Corps Commander, paid us a visit.

The officers had a Brigade Club in the village where they exchanged gossip (and perhaps drinks), and the N.C.O.'s had a very good Mess. Christmas Day was celebrated in fine style by all ranks—plenty of all good things to eat and drink for officers and men. In addressing the Battalion, the Brigadier said:

"Looking back on the year 1916, the most critical year of this War, we can only do so with pride. As a Division we have had a longer period on the Somme than any other Division in the Army. . . . . . This Brigade of the three Brigades in this Division has been most severely put to the test, and we have had several more weeks in the trenches than the other Brigades. The Hallamshires were the first, or nearly the first, in it on the 1st July, and we had to take over the "A" Line and stay there under the most trying conditions. Continually, during the period we were on the Somme, the Hallamshires were suffering the heaviest casualties. No one could have shown better spirit than the Hallamshires right through. I always think, when I want to see how a thing should be done, and I am not certain about it, 'I'll go round to the Hallamshires and see how they do it.' Anyhow, if this spirit carries on, I cannot ask for anything better. The spirit carried on under fire should be carried on during training, and I feel that you all realise what is before us. This next year's fighting depends upon you, and you cannot take it too much to heart. Up to now we have only been allowed to go over the parapet in small parties, and we will hope in the coming year to go over the parapet again as a Brigade, and I feel confident that no other Brigade in the British Army will carry out what it is asked to do better than the 148th Brigade, and that the Hallamshires will distinguish themselves in the Brigade."

On New Year's Day, 1917, Brigade Competitions were held in (1) Ceremonial Drill and General Turnout; (2) Shooting; (3) Lewis Gun Work; (4) Football.

No. 1 was won by the Hallamshires (2nd Lieutenant H. R. Dixon and No. 5 Platoon).

1917. JANUARY.

No. 2 by the Hallamshires (2nd Lieutenant H. S. Ackernley and No. 3 Platoon).

No. 3 by the 5th K.O.Y.L.I., and

No. 4 by the Hallamshires.

2nd Lieutenant H. S. Ackernley and No. 3 Platoon also won the Divisional Shooting Competition on the following day, and on the 4th January 2nd Lieutenant H. R. Dixon won the Divisional Competition in Ceremonial with No. 5 Platoon.

CHAPTER VII

RANSART

(See Map 2)

COLONEL WYATT returned from leave on January 2nd and assumed temporary command of the 146th Brigade, leaving Major Branson, who had been in charge during his absence, still in command of the Hallamshires. On the 3rd the C.O., Adjutant and Company Commanders went up to reconnoitre the Ransart sector, and two days later the villagers turned out *en masse* to cheer us as we marched out of Sus-St. Leger for the line. During our stay in Sus-St. Leger every item of equipment had been polished up to a state of perfection. Our steel helmets were painted a gorgeous yellow, with the badge of the Regiment in front, and their glossiness almost made the General purr as we marched past him. Later in the day, however, when he passed us halted by the roadside, and he saw almost every man in the Battalion using his 18-carat tin hat as a seat, his wrath was terrible to behold! Possibly the General had never had occasion to discover that the inside of a tin hat is infinitely more comfortable as a seat than the sharp cobbles and mud of the roadside!

On arrival in the forward area the Battalion relieved the 18th Manchesters (30th Division)—B Company (Captain P. N. Johnson), D Company (Captain J. E. D. Stickney), and Battalion Headquarters in Bailleulval, with A Company (Captain H. K. Wilson) and C Company (Captain J. F. Wortley) in the neighbouring village of Basseux. The strength of the Battalion on January 5th was 32 officers and 1,005 O.R.

On January 6th we moved up into the line, relieving the 17th Manchesters. Once again the Battalion settled down to regular trench routine, and if it were not for Captain Johnson's raid, the arrival of detachments of the London Regiment for instruction, and the booming of the SECTION, our stay in Ransart could be dismissed very speedily.

The Battalion moved from the trenches in front of Grosville to Bellacourt (in support), back to the trenches in front of Grosville, and thence into Brigade Reserve at Bailleulval and Basseux in rotation, staying in each position some five or six days.

1917. JANUARY.

The trenches were held with three companies in the line, and Battalion Headquarters and one company in Grosville. As at Hébuterne, each company held Lewis-gun and bombing posts, with the remainder of the company in close support. The trenches were very wet and the cold was soon intense. By the time the Battalion's second turn for the trenches came round, there had been a heavy fall of snow and the ground was frozen hard. After using gum-boots throughout the winter, it was a positive pleasure to go into the line in ankle boots and puttees. Any damage to the trenches, however, was extremely difficult to repair, as even a pick-axe would not pierce the ground. It was not uncommon for an enemy time-fuze shell to strike the ground and ricochet for some distance before exploding. Moreover, having discovered some of the tracks in the snow made by officers and runners from company headquarters to the front line, the enemy swept them with frequent bursts of machine gun fire. On the whole, the situation was very quiet, and even when, as frequently occurred, our artillery bombarded strong points in the enemy's line, there was practically no retaliation.

The support company, of course, supplied working parties for the front line companies, and the weather was so cold that everyone worked hard to keep warm. Battalion Headquarters were very comfortably billeted in a farm-house in Grosville itself. Although it stood practically at the entrance to a main communication trench and not more than 1,500 yards from the enemy, this farm was still occupied by civilians, of whom there were a number in the village. On one occasion a small girl was selling flags at the entrance to the communication trench, and was only prevented by the regimental police from going up into the line. The "flag day" was in aid of a fund for the relief of consumptive French soldiers, and this enterprising little flapper reaped quite a rich harvest from Battalion Headquarters and the support company.

There was a diversion on February 2nd, when Battalion Headquarters and C Company of the 2/3rd London Regiment arrived at Grosville to be introduced to war. Each platoon was attached to one of our companies. As their Battalion Headquarters alone consisted of some ten officers, and as each of their officers was equipped with all the customary "indispensable" articles, the problem of accommodation and commissariat presented considerable difficulty, but they were made as comfortable as possible. Later on similar parties from the 2/1st and 2/10th Londons were attached in the same way. It was fortunate that the enemy was not at all offensively inclined during their visit, as the trenches were packed with men, and heavy shelling would certainly have caused many casualties.

When on duty in Brigade Reserve one company held four strong posts (Boundary, Orchard, Star Fish and Burnt Farm) in Grosville, while the rest of the Battalion occupied billets in the village of Bellacourt, when it was not providing working parties for Battalions in the line. The four posts were part of the "Divisional Line." They were built on sites specially selected for their command of ground, and were very strongly wired. Each post held its own reserve of food, water and ammunition, and in the event of an enemy break-through they would have been very serious obstacles to him. The garrison of each post consisted of one platoon. The headquarters of the company finding the garrisons occupied a house in the war-worn village of Bretencourt.

* * * * * *

If the business of holding the line in the Ransart sector was mainly defensive, the work of the Battalion in Brigade Reserve in the villages of Bailleulval and Basseux was almost entirely offensive, even to the frequent conferences at the Officers' Club at Basseux!

The training was INTENSIVE in every way. Particular attention was paid to the training of platoon and section commanders in specialist work and tactics. Everything was based on the discovery that the section was the unit which mattered, and the efforts to keep every section (even in the line) at the standard strength of "1 N.C.O. and 6" caused Company Commanders and Adjutant almost as much excitement as an election count! On January 30th each company in turn gave an exhibition of the assault on specially constructed trenches at Basseux; but Company Commanders afterwards sought consolation in the fact that real assaults are not usually made under the closely critical eyes of the Brigade Staff.

In the meantime, 2nd Lieutenant W. D. G. Gifford (the Scout Officer) had not been idle. He had observed that the Boche was in the habit of repairing his wire defences just before dawn, and the C.O. therefore drew up a scheme to secure an "identification" which was urgently needed. In the dark hour before dawn on February 5th a party of nineteen ghosts might have been seen crawling about on the snow in "No Man's Land." By 5-30 a.m. the ghosts (Gifford and eighteen men) were in position. The idea was for our artillery to open out suddenly on the spot where the enemy was in the habit of carrying out his wiring practice, and then Gifford and his merry men would rush out and secure the body of any wounded or dead Boche. Zero hour was 6 a.m., when our artillery fired a hurricane burst of shrapnel on the enemy. After two minutes the artillery lifted and the party rushed in. The Boche was not in an obliging mood just then, apparently, for nothing but wire and shell holes were found, and the party returned to our lines empty-handed.

A little later the Authorities decided that a raid on a larger scale was necessary, and a chosen party, consisting of Captain P. N. Johnson, M.C., Lieutenants H. R. Dixon, T. A. Merry, and about eighty other ranks, were sent back to Bailleulval for training. The actual raid was practised several times over ground specially prepared and marked out to represent the enemy lines. Every detail was carefully worked out and each man thoroughly coached in his own particular job.

* * * * * *

A communiqué from General Headquarters dated 18/2/17 stated :—

"We entered the German positions during the night South-West and also North-West of Arras, South of Fauquissart, and North of Ypres. We inflicted many casualties on the enemy, blew up a machine gun, and brought back nineteen prisoners."

A German communiqué of the same date said :—

"After lively artillery preparation, strong English reconnoitring detachments endeavoured to force their way into our trenches North of Armentières and South-West of Lille, and likewise North of the La Bassée Canal and near Ransart. They were repulsed partly by hand-to-hand fighting (during which prisoners fell into our hands) and partly by our fire."

These simple (and contradictory!) statements give but a slight idea of what these operations mean to the troops taking part.

A raid is a complete attack on a small scale, with the addition of the risks of withdrawal from the captured position; and the chances of success are limited because time is limited and details have to be worked out with such precision that a slight accident may be enough to set the whole delicate machinery out of gear. There is no second chance.

The object of the raid was to obtain an identification and to inflict casualties by entering the enemy trenches at the Blockhouse at two points about forty yards apart, and dealing with the garrison on arrival.

The enemy wire had been engaged by our 18-pounders and medium and heavy T.M.'s for several days, but it was thought that it had not been completely cut, and it was therefore necessary to take a party of sappers with bangalore torpedoes to be used if required.

The force was divided into two raiding parties, each consisting of an officer and 25 other ranks, two flanking parties to prevent the enemy from cutting off the force in "No Man's Land," two covering parties to prevent the enemy from disturbing the operation by sending reinforcements down his front line, and a supporting party under Captain Johnson.

A varied assortment of weapons was carried, including rifles, bayonets, Mills bombs, phosphorus bombs, wire-cutters, knobkerries, revolvers, flash lamps and razors, the last-named for cutting off shoulder-straps for identification purposes.

It was arranged that the covering parties should leave our lines forty minutes before zero (which was fixed for 10 p.m.), followed twenty minutes later by the remainder. The artillery were to open on the front line at zero hour, and immediately the sappers, with the raiding and covering parties, were to get forward to the wire, cut it, and lie down as close as possible to the barrage inside the wire and report when they were ready to assault. Tapes were to be laid through the gaps to facilitate the withdrawal. If no message was received, the barrage was to lift in sixteen minutes.

The frost had held for more than a month, but on the 16th there was a decided thaw and the trenches were speedily transformed into their more familiar state. Rain fell heavily during the afternoon of the raid, and there were frequent showers throughout the night, which was very dark.

About an hour before zero there was a strange noise in "No Man's Land," and a voice could be heard quite clearly calling out, "Tommy! Tommy! Come and help me, Tommy—I'm wounded!" Search was made very cautiously, but the voice could not be located exactly. This may have been a trick to lure one of our men into a trap, but all were too busy to pay much attention, although sentries were warned to be particularly on the alert.

The bad weather made it difficult to reach the assembly position in the middle of "No Man's Land," and it was not until 10-10 p.m. that Johnson was able to inform the C.O. that all had arrived there.

1917. FEBRUARY.

The barrage was falling nicely on the Germans' front line, and, under cover of this, the raiders moved forward and exploded the bangalore torpedoes successfully. At 10-15 p.m., however, Johnson 'phoned the C.O. to say that he had received no reports as to the cutting of the wire (they eventually got through at 10-25 and 10-32), and the C.O. arranged with the artillery to extend the bombardment. At 10-32 Johnson 'phoned for the barrage to lift.

The two attacking parties at once entered the enemy trenches. The right party soon found a dug-out, and the Germans were ordered to come out. Two of them came up the steps and then turned back. They were promptly shot, when the remainder, twelve in number, came up quietly and were taken prisoners and sent back to the supports. The left party had a somewhat similar experience. They also were compelled to shoot a couple of Huns before the remainder would leave their dug-out. This party brought back six prisoners, making eighteen in all, but as one of the enemy taken by the right party became troublesome during his walk across "No Man's Land," they were compelled to dispose of him, thus reducing the total bag to seventeen.

Lieutenant Merry and his men were later in returning to our lines than were the left party, and this caused considerable anxiety for a short time. At 11-10 p.m., however, the artillery ceased fire, and by 11-15 p.m. all our men were back in our lines.

The enemy trenches had been almost demolished, several Germans had been killed, and seventeen brought safely back to our lines at a total cost of two men very slightly wounded. The prisoners were taken first of all to Battalion Headquarters in the farm-house at Grosville, and the scene in the Mess was memorable. The room was a very large one, with a big plain wooden table in the centre. All round the walls were the Boche prisoners, some looking very surly, whilst others had an expression of indescribable relief. One of the happy ones was a mere boy of some seventeen or eighteen years. The prisoners were then sent down to Brigade Headquarters under an escort; the remainder of our raiding party returned to Bailleulval and bed: the C.O. sat down to make out his report on the raid; and the Adjutant stood with the telephone glued to his ear taking congratulatory messages and answering the Staff Captain's anxious enquiries as to the number of pairs of socks changed during the previous day!

The raid was in every way a success. It had been carefully pre-

1917. FEBRUARY.

pared, splendidly carried out, and the prisoners taken provided the information required.

The decorations awarded for the raid were as follows :—

Military Cross. 2nd Lieutenant W. D. G. Gifford, for his excellent preparatory scouting work, which contributed largely to the successful result.

D.C.M. C.S.M. W. Pemberton.

M.M. Sergeant J. Kay, Corporal T. F. Hayes, Lance-Corporal A. P. Tarlton, Lance-Corporal A. G. Seabrooke, Private F. Lymer, Private A. Vernon.

The Brigadier presented ribbons to the above a few days later, and during his speech he remarked upon the unique record of the Hallamshires in being "foremost on the football field, on the drill ground, at the rifle range, and in 'No Man's Land.' "

* * * * * *

The day after the raid the Battalion was relieved by the 4th K.O.Y.L.I. and marched into Divisional Reserve at Bailleulval. The first day was spent, as usual, in cleaning up. Rumours of a move from the Ransart sector were in the air, and the men worked hard to get clean and smart. Until February 23rd the companies carried out general training in the fields near Bailleulval, except on February 20th, when A and D Companies paid a farewell visit to this part of the line to work for the 147th Brigade Trench Mortar Battery. The attached company of the London Regiment had concluded its period of instruction, and left us on February 19th, and the line was now held by the 58th Division.

On February 14th Captain Bernard left to take up an appointment with the XVIII. Corps Cavalry, being succeeded by Lieutenant J. W. Elliott, R.A.M.C., as Battalion Medical Officer. We were all very sorry to lose the Doctor. He had been with us for eighteen months, and was liked and respected by the men as he was beloved by the officers. Any man who was really ill knew that in Captain Bernard he would find a friend as well as a doctor, but the professional "lead-swinger" knew that he could not practise his art without being at once discovered. Whether we were in or out of the trenches, the "Doc" did not consider that his work began and ended by attending to the sick at Battalion Headquarters, and dealing with casualties, and when there was "something doing" he was always to the fore. He was the best Mess President Battalion Headquarters ever had, and his extraordinary geniality made life there very pleasant.

CHAPTER VIII

NEUVE CHAPELLE

(See Maps 2 and 1)

" . . . . . . In most of the spheres of war the first quarter of 1917 saw the reaping of harvests sown by other hands. The deferred dividends on the Somme campaign were paid, and the Germans fell back from hundreds of square miles of French territory."—Professor A. F. Pollard in " A Short History of the Great War."

COLONEL WYATT rejoined us from the 146th Brigade on February 23rd, and the next day the Battalion marched to Gaudiempré, a distance of 7 or 8 kilometres. At this time the enemy was making his famous withdrawal "according to plan," and the C.O. was constantly receiving telegrams, which made it uncertain whether we should have to return to the Ransart sector to help in the chase. On February 25th we marched N.W. for 15 kilometres, and were billeted at Ivergny for two very peaceful days.

On February 28th we marched to Bouquemaison, only 5 kilos south of Ivergny—apparently for no reason other than that some other unit wanted the billets we then occupied, but, as a matter of fact, we were so comfortable at Bouquemaison that we were sorry only to stay there one night.

At 9 o'clock the following morning we paraded on the road with our faces turned to the north, and a few minutes later the whole Brigade was on the march, making a very good show. We covered more than 17 kilometres before reaching our destination, a pretty little village called Croisette. H.Q. stayed with the Curé, and were regaled with a home-made but powerful liqueur, the foundation of which was honey. Early next morning we marched for Floringhem *via* St. Pol and Pernes. Most of the route was a first-class road, and although the distance covered was 21 kilometres, the Battalion finished in splendid condition.

Whilst the column was passing through St. Pol there was a block in the traffic in front of us, which caused our Battalion to halt on a steep hill. This block put a heavy strain on our transport animals, but it was even more unfortunate that a car containing the Army Commander was held up immediately in rear of us. General Allenby appeared to think that we had halted on that terrible hill for a drink

1917. MARCH.

or a smoke, for he leaned out of his car and ordered the nearest officer to clear the obstruction. The officer addressed happened to be Lieutenant Elliott, our new Medical Officer, who merely saluted, answered "Yes, Sir," and began to make his way in the direction of the head of the Battalion as fast as his 3 m.p.h. pony would take him.

Staying successive nights at Floringhem and St. Floris, we reached the village of Bout de Ville on the evening of March 4th. Within a few minutes of leaving Floringhem we had marched "off the map" (Lens 11), on which we had worked for so long that most officers knew it better than that of their native county in England.

During all this long trek, often over very bad roads, in full marching order, and wearing steel helmets, the Battalion marched splendidly, and only one man fell out. The Band worked like heroes, and were a great help to us—except when they played "The Lads of Killiecrankie," which they invariably raced through at 160 to the minute!

On the last day of the march Colonel Wyatt, with the Adjutant and four Company Commanders, went ahead by motor lorry and looked round the line in the Neuve Chapelle sector, which we were to take over. After the strenuous marches of the past four days the men anticipated at least one day's rest, but were doomed to disappointment. By 9 a.m. the following day every man was clear of Bout de Ville *en route* for the trenches in a blinding snowstorm.

The Battalion relieved the 8th Middlesex Regiment (56th Division) in daylight. The trenches were in fair condition, but were very wet. The high ground of the Aubers Ridge was directly in front of us, and as our area was almost dead flat, we realised that water was to be reckoned among our chief troubles. The Brigade sector was divided into two battalion sectors, the 5th York and Lancaster Regiment being on the right and the Hallamshires on the left. Battalion Headquarters were at an old farm called Winchester House, with various dug-outs near by for Orderly Room and Battalion Headquarters Staff. The sector was held by three companies in the line and one in strong posts in the vicinity of Battalion Headquarters.

The enemy was very quiet at first, but we soon found that he had a number of heavy trench mortars which were likely to be troublesome. These threw a huge shell containing more than 200lbs. of high explosive, and inspired a very healthy respect. The noise of the mortar firing the shell was rather like the pop of a champagne cork, and could be heard distinctly from our lines, while the devastation caused by a direct hit on our trench gave us work for days, and sometimes made it necessary to rebuild our line in front of, or behind, the huge crater made by the shell.

Our front line contained entrances to several big mines, on which our Mining Companies had been working for years. As the enemy was similarly employed, we never knew what was going to happen.

The Scout Officer and his men very soon began to make "No Man's Land" our property, and they had some exciting nights before they quite mastered the geography of it. We spent six days in the line, and were then relieved by the 4th K.O.Y.L.I. Our casualties during the tour were one man killed and seven wounded.

(a) The "Situation Quiet."

On relief, we marched into the village of Pont du Hem, where we were delighted to find good billets in the farms and houses. Although but a few thousand yards from the line, the inhabitants were still "carrying on" as if the Boche were a hundred miles away.

On March 17th Colonel Wyatt, who had been in indifferent health for several weeks, was persuaded to go into hospital. He was eventually sent to England, and on his recovery was posted as Second-in-Command to Brigadier-General Kentish at the Senior Officer's School at Aldershot. He returned to France again in time to fight in the great retreat of March, 1918, as Brigadier-General Commanding "Wyatt's Mixed Force."

We now began a fairly regular life of six days "in" and six days "out," nearly always at Pont du Hem. When in this village we always occupied the same billets, and were able to make ourselves comfortable in many ways.

It was a very happy thought which prompted the authorities to allow us to relieve, and be relieved by, the 4th K.O.Y.L.I. throughout our stay in this area. By this means, what was so frequently a troublesome and complicated business when dealing with a battalion new to the sector, became quite a pleasant social incident.

On March 29th, on going into the line, our front was extended so that our right company now held the famous "Duck's Bill" Crater—a huge mine-crater filled with water to a depth of many feet. This was in "No Man's Land," but we held it day and night. We had a sap leading up to it, and a bombing post and Lewis-gun post built in the sap-head. The rim of the crater had a low barbed-wire fence round

1917. MARCH.

to prevent men from falling into the water in the dark—as several men had been drowned there in the past. At night it was a most eerie place, and no one whose duty did not compel him would linger there, but during the day it was a means of providing a mild excitement for the many "visitors," Staff or otherwise, who passed along that sector of trench. Visitors of the thoughtless type were apt to make a little too much noise and show a little too much head when moving up the narrow sap to the crater. The result, of course, was that the observant Hun would report "much movement" in the vicinity of the crater, and it would be treated to a good dose of trench mortars—after the visitors had gone home.

We caused a slight flutter in the dovecote of the engineers by indenting for a life-buoy. Rumour says that the indent went through to General Headquarters, whence it was transferred to the Admiralty. However that may be, the life-buoy arrived in due course, to be marked "H.M.S. Queen" (our code name at the time) and hung up by the side of the water.

Work in the line consisted largely of drainage, and, helped by an improvement in the weather, good progress was made. The fall of the land was about 1½ inches per 1,000 yards, and it would have taxed the skill of a battalion of civil engineers to clear the trenches of water. However, we did our best with pumps, shovels and scoops, and soon had the satisfaction of being able to walk the length of the front line dry-shod.

From Pont du Hem we provided large working parties—usually three companies—every night. These parties had to march up and work for four or five hours—sometimes more—in the trenches. The result was that officers and men were in the front trenches, either holding the line or on working parties, almost every day during the three and a half months we were in the Neuve Chapelle area.

Generally speaking, the situation was quiet, though the enemy made many opportunities for rude interruptions. One of his favourite methods of reminding us of his feelings towards us took the form of "Granatenwerfer." These are light trench mortars fired very rapidly, and were known variously as "pineapples," "vane bombs," or "aerial darts." However, we found an effective way of retaliating by fixing up rifle-grenade batteries and sending the Boche six rifle grenades for each Granatenwerfer bomb.

On April 1st, a Sunday, we were given the usual strafe—for some occult reason the German always used up his spare ammunition on Sundays and Wednesdays—but only three men were wounded. Snow fell next day, and made the trenches rather unpleasant, but it cleared away quickly under the warm sun, and we soon got the water out, as our drains were running very well now. In the afternoon the enemy made a determined attempt to smash up one of our medium trench mortars ("Footballs") which had evidently been annoying him. Sixty heavy shells were rained on to the spot, but the mortar was not touched, although one front line parapet was blown about and North Tilleloy St. communication trench was quite flattened out at the front line end. We suffered no casualties, as the officer on duty moved his men to a flank until the bombardment was over.

Colonel Branson's appointment to the command was made on the 3rd April, and Major J. E. D. Stickney became Second-in-Command.

On April 26th we were heavily strafed with gas shells, and had to stand-to for an hour or so with our respirators adjusted; while on May 6th we had a severe shock. At about 7 p.m. there was scarcely a sound to be heard in the front line except the croaking of frogs in the water-logged craters of "No Man's Land." Suddenly a great flame shot up on our left. This was followed by a terrific report, and the trenches quaked like jelly. A huge column of black smoke rose into the sky, and it appeared that the enemy had exploded a mine under our lines. As a matter of fact, the explosion had taken place just behind the left flank of our Battalion—and had been caused by a trench-mortar man who, whilst working on Stokes shells, had lost his nerve and thrown a fused shell on to a dump of three hundred others. The explosion completely wrecked our front line for a distance of fifty yards.

The 2nd May was a perfect spring day. In the afternoon it was quite hot, and everyone was taking things quietly in Pont du Hem. There was the usual desultory gun fire, but the grimness of war was not at all evident. The men were lying about round and inside their billets reading and writing letters, while here and there an orderly sergeant or corporal was reading out the detail for the night working parties. Suddenly the peacefulness was disturbed by the droning of a big shell—there was a tremendous crash, and then a crackling as of a thousand rifles. The officers rushed from the Club to see huge flames shooting out of a billet on the main La Bassée road. Help was given to any man who needed it, but the big shell—an 8-inch—had dropped into the middle of a barn in which about thirty men of B Company were having tea. Twelve were killed outright and sixteen wounded—several seriously. The wounded were put into a motor lorry, which had been stopped and commandeered for the purpose, and in less than half an hour they were in hospital. Instructions had been issued some time before as to the action to be taken in case of the village being shelled, and as the shelling continued at the rate of about two shells per minute, the men were rapidly moved to open areas on the flanks. From 4-30 p.m. to 7-45 p.m. some 350 eight-inch shells fell on the immediate area of the farm. It is a remarkable thing that only the first, which hit the farm, did any damage.

In the orchard of the farm were hidden a couple of sixty-pounder guns. These had been chased about from place to place for some time. They had been put into the orchard during the preceding night, were screened entirely from overhead view, and had not fired a single round since reaching the orchard. The guns themselves escaped injury, except that one was slightly damaged by a fragment of shell, but the orchard and ground round the farm suffered severely.

In the late evening of April 13th the enemy exploded a small mine, which did no damage.

In February Major M. J. Duggan left the Battalion for duty at the Base Signal Depôt. His services to the Battalion, both in peace and in war, had been invaluable. There may have been a better Quartermaster in the British Army, but those who served with him doubt it.

(b) The Portuguese.

Not the least important of our tasks in the Neuve Chapelle sector was the instruction of Portuguese. We have been called upon to act as teachers of warfare to English and American troops—but the Portuguese were a tougher proposition altogether. Apart from the language difficulty, they had special rations and their organisation differed from ours. They were entirely ignorant of the Western Front type of warfare, and were badly equipped in some respects—*e.g.*, they had only one Lewis gun per company of 200 men. However, the first company arrived on April 10th. We split it up among the Battalion, and hoped for the best.

The men of the Hallamshires seemed thoroughly to enjoy the experience. The Portuguese soldier broke almost every regulation in the trench code, but it was of little use to remonstrate with him in English, and the attached interpreter was usually somewhere else when one found a man playing with the safety pins of Mills bombs!

1917. April—May.

On the other hand, their keenness was embarrassing at times, as at least one Hallamshire ration-carrier had cause to know. A Portuguese sentry, acting on the principle of "seeing without being seen," etc., challenged with the bayonet only—and the ration-carrier was saved by a loaf of bread in the sack he was carrying in front of him! It was about this time that a sergeant, when asked by the Divisional Commander how he got on with the Portuguese, replied: "Not bad, Sir, but it would be much better if they could talk French." The quality of the sergeant's own French may be imagined!

Later on we had two more companies attached to us at the same time, and though we did our best for them, it was rather a strain for one battalion to be responsible for 400 novices. On this occasion Captain Wortley had a company commander attached to him who could not speak a single word of either English or French. Apparently he misunderstood the meaning of the word "attached," for on leaving Captain Wortley he embraced him and kissed him on both cheeks in front of many of the men!

On May 19th a Portuguese Commanding Officer, with his Second-in-Command, Adjutant and Company Commanders, joined us in the trenches; and the Platoon Commanders arrived on the following day for twenty-four hours' special instruction before taking over the line. The complete 24th Portuguese Battalion arrived, according to programme, on the 21st May, and, considering the language difficulty, the relief was carried out very satisfactorily. We left a stiffening of our officers, N.C.O.'s and observers with the Portuguese.

(c) *More Raids.*

Early in the morning of the 9th April we heard the distant booming of our guns, which heralded the Canadian assault and capture of Vimy Ridge. The ridge could be quite plainly seen from our front line.

This desire to worry the enemy appeared to be troubling our Scout Officer, too, for he rapidly acquired a useful knowledge of the Boche front line, which he used almost as freely as our own, as it appeared that it was very seldom manned by sentries. During our first tour in this sector he found a steel and concrete machine gun emplacement in the enemy line, and the "Gilded Ones" decided that it must be blown up, and so he took out fourteen men on the night of February 18th and blew the offender into the sky. The next night he

1917. MAY.
again visited the enemy front line and fixed a wire to the parapet with a view to over-hearing enemy telephone messages.

On another occasion (May 9th) he took out a patrol to a point near the German support line, where they fixed up a notice-board, written in German, inviting the enemy to come over to our lines and surrender. The troops opposing us were German-Poles, and it was thought that the invitation might bring some of them over, but they ignored it, and did not even trouble to remove the notice-board, which could be seen from our lines.

On May 7th the Battalion on our left carried out a raid at 9-40 p.m., and we put up a "dummy" show in conjunction with it. A party of fifty men, under Lieutenant J. S. Houlton, was sent into the Birdcage Craters in "No Man's Land," where Lieutenant Williams, with two Stokes mortar teams, joined him. At zero they brought enfilade fire from Stokes mortars and rifle grenades to bear upon the German front line and certain other selected spots. Meanwhile, Lieutenant Gifford took eighteen scouts across the Boche line in a direction away from our fire, and made a careful survey of the enemy preserves. The front line trenches were found to be in a very bad state, and contained about two feet of water. Gifford penetrated further into the lines, but saw no sign of the enemy, and there is no doubt that he had abandoned his front line because of its water-logged condition. We withdrew our parties without a single casualty, although the enemy sent down a heavy retaliatory shoot.

There was a small wood on our right front, the Bois du Biez—popularly known as "Mystery Wood." This was certainly the home of several heavy trench mortars, and it was so dense that it would have been possible for the enemy to assemble a large number of men there. It was rumoured that the R.E.'s were to burn the wood down, but in the end it was decided to give it instead a good soaking of the gas which had been so successful further south. As usual with gas "stunts," the operation had been ordered several times and cancelled owing to a change in the direction of the wind, but at 11 p.m. on May 8th the gas was sent over by firing several hundred cylinders from "projectors" simultaneously. There was a loud explosion and a huge sheet of flame several hundred feet high, and then a great cloud of gas could be seen rolling steadily on the wood. To add to the demoralising effect, each of our three heavy trench mortars dropped ten "flying pigs" on the Boche lines. The enemy retaliated with artillery and trench mortars, but did very little material damage and caused no casualties. It was known later that the enemy sustained several hundred casualties and was compelled to relieve his troops in that sector.

Our Stokes mortars had a special hurricane shoot on May 18th; and on the 25th the Engineers fired a "camouflet" in "No Man's Land," the subterranean explosion causing a minor earthquake in our lines.

In the early morning of June 3rd the Germans raided the Portuguese in the vicinity of the Duck's Bill Crater and extracted ten prisoners. Hence we were not surprised to hear next day that we were to carry out in reply a raid on a large scale. The details were rapidly arranged, and the party selected spent its time practising the raid on ground near Rue Bacquerot, a mile behind our front line trenches.

The party consisted of about two hundred and forty men under ten officers, with Major Stickney in command. The plan was to advance from the Birdcage Craters in a south-east direction, with the right on the German front line and the left a hundred yards inside his territory (which was believed to be held by isolated posts only), to kill or capture any Germans met, and to do as much damage as possible to the German trenches.

Two or three nights before the raid Lieutenants Ryan, Gifford, Martin and Bridger went up to the line for a final reconnaissance. They penetrated some considerable distance beyond the enemy front line, and were then suddenly challenged in German. Several shots were fired at them, but they got back safely to our lines with a very useful knowledge of the enemy ground.

Zero hour was fixed for 12-30 a.m. on the night of June 11/12th. The afternoon of the 11th was spent busily at La Fosse in settling the many necessary details (very similar, of course, to those described in Chapter VII.), and then the party was inspected by the General. In a short speech he intimated that our raid, besides having great importance of its own, was necessary in order to divert a little enemy attention from the battle which was then going on at Messines, and that on receiving instructions that his Brigade was to make the raid, he had selected the Hallamshires, feeling confident that they would succeed.

The party was then packed into motor lorries and drove off. If the enemy had any spies at all on our side of the line, he must have been aware that something was on foot, for the string of about ten lorries, packed with black-faced men, passed through four or five vil-

1917. JUNE.

lages full of open-mouthed civilians. Near Epinette Dump they picked up bangalore torpedoes and the sappers who were to fire them, and then made themselves comfortable near the foot of the communication trenches and rested for an hour or so, as there was plenty of time to spare before they could go up to the front line. The Portuguese troops, in the part of the line concerned, had been withdrawn, and Captain P. N. Johnson, with B Company, took over in their stead. When it was dark enough, the raiders moved off up the winding communication trench and began to file out over the top to take up the positions of assembly. A good deal of water-logged ground was anticipated, and, therefore, each of the four front-line platoons carried a specially-made bridge for crossing any impassable places.

At 12-27 a.m. everyone was in position, and the seconds dragged slowly along until 12-30, when the whole front appeared to break into flame, and down came the barrage. The raid had been practised so carefully that when the time came all were exactly in the positions laid down—*i.e.,* fifty yards from where the barrage should have fallen. This distance has been proved many times to be perfectly safe, and it has the obvious advantage of allowing our attacking troops to be on top of the enemy when the barrage lifts before he has time to recover himself. Unfortunately, however, in this case one of the batteries was not shooting accurately, and, within five minutes of zero, one of our shells burst just behind Lieutenant Ryan and a shrapnel bullet passed through his thigh. Next minute a shell burst amongst a Lewis-gun section, killing or wounding every man and blowing the gun to pieces. Other platoons fared little better. In spite of these difficulties, and now very much reduced in strength, the raiders pressed on, and twenty minutes after zero the left company (Captain E. M. Holmes) sent down two prisoners, while soon after 1 a.m. the right company (Captain S. Brooke) sent eleven more to Headquarters. By this time casualties were so heavy that it was realised that every remaining man would be required for carrying in the wounded. Of Lieutenant Ryan's platoon of thirty-one men there remained only three unwounded. Major Stickney then sent every available man from the supports and also the men of the right party who were returning, up to the left to assist in clearing the casualties. Lieutenant O'Donnell was found very seriously wounded and was carried back, but died on reaching our lines. The work of clearing the casualties was continued until dawn arrived, and made it impossible to remain out any longer, but by this time all the wounded and most of the dead had been brought in. Padre Elgood had been out during the whole of the time helping to carry the wounded to our lines.

The enemy retaliation was not very serious. He trench-mortared his own front line mercilessly, but most of the party were well past it by the time he began to shoot. The raid was a success from a military point of view, as we had achieved our object and secured thirteen prisoners, one of whom was a "Hauptmann." The cost, however, had been very great. We lost twenty-eight men killed and fifty-five wounded; and of the officers, O'Donnell was killed and Ryan and Williams were wounded.

The inaccurate artillery fire which had caused most of our casualties was traced to a Portuguese battery. Our own artillery officers had registered the guns of the Portuguese accurately, and every possible precaution had been taken by our artillery commander, but, despite this, the Portuguese altered their ranges at the last moment without reference to our C.R.A., and thus caused the loss of many valuable lives.

The mining company working from our lines provided us with an exciting little side-show in connection with the raid. On June 10th we learned that our miners, working from a shaft running from the Chord (a trench nearly opposite the sector to be raided), had broken into a German gallery. During the raid Sergeant Jackson and a dozen men explored the whole of this gallery under "No Man's Land," and came to the surface in the enemy front line. Unfortunately, there were no Germans about for them to capture, but this party gave very valuable assistance in guiding our casualties back under cover through the gallery and tunnel. This gallery was also used during the raid by General Adlercron, who always preferred personal observation to second-hand reports, and the risks of the front line to the safety of Brigade Headquarters during a scrap.

For gallantry during the raid the *Military Cross* was awarded to Captain E. M. Holmes, Captain S. Brooke, and the Reverend H. F. Elgood; the *Distinguished Conduct Medal* to Sergeants G. H. Beedham and A. Jones; and the *Military Medal* to Lance-Sergeant W. D. Galley, Privates J. Smith, J. Longden, T. McAvoy and W. Tyler.

* * * * * *

We returned to La Fosse after the raid. Our Battalion strength was then thirty-five officers and nearly nine hundred men, and after moving to Bout de Ville on June 24th we received a draft of four more officers; 2nd Lieutenant E. Williams rejoined us from the T.M. Battery, and forty-seven O.R. arrived to be divided between the companies which had lost most heavily in the raid.

During the week at Bout de Ville the last party (5 officers and 50 men) lent to the Portuguese returned to us; and working parties were provided every night.

Early in the morning of July 1st the Battalion moved to La Gorgue, where our transport lines and Q.M. stores had been situated since March 5th. Captain Harold Steel rejoined us here. For the next few days we carried out training under company arrangements—also under great difficulties owing to lack of ground suitable for training.

The Brigade Sports and Horse Show were held on the 11th July at Bout de Ville. Our animals were not of a sufficiently high class to win medals, but the excellence of the grooming and turn-out reflected great credit upon our Transport Officer and his men. In the Brigade Cross-Country Run the Battalion carried all before it, securing the first three places. Sergeant Shute was the first in at the finish.

CHAPTER IX

NIEUPORT

(See Map 3)

ON July 8th two companies went to the Brigade School at Les Caudrons for specialist training. The rest of the Battalion moved to Vieille Chapelle, relieving the 5th Y. and L. "Alice's," at the latter village, was a popular resort for a day or two, but on July 10th the two companies at Les Caudrons rejoined owing to the prospect of a sudden move, and next day the Battalion marched to Beuvry, near Béthune.

We left the Neuve Chapelle sector with mingled feelings. We had been very comfortable, but we were very tired of the routine. Everything at Neuve Chapelle had been done "according to the book," and the trenches were held and kept so efficiently that the war might have continued for a century without either side obtaining any decisive advantage. We all felt that it was time to stop dusting the parapet, and to get on with the war; and after we left the Neuve Chapelle sector this stereotyped system of warfare never recurred.

After a couple of days at Beuvry the Battalion entrained at 4 p.m. on the 13th July at Béthune Station for Dunkerque, arriving there at 1 a.m. next day. From Dunkerque the Battalion was conveyed by barges up the canal to Rosendael, where we relieved the 2/10th Manchesters on the coast defences. On the 16th we handed over to the 8th West Yorks. and marched to Coxyde with a view to taking over the trenches in the St. George's sector, but the orders were altered and we took over the line from the 15th Lancashire Fusiliers in the right half of the Lombartzyde sector, just east of Nieuport.

The Messines-Wytschaete ridge had been captured in June, and our long rest from active operations led us to suppose that we were not going into Belgium merely to hold the line. The concentration of heavy guns, which we discovered in the Lombartzyde sector, only confirmed our suspicions, but on our way north the news had come through that the Germans, anticipating trouble, had made a defensive thrust on July 10th, capturing two British battalions and a large slice of ground near the coast. This, of course, upset all plans, and we were put into the line, to suffer in eight days almost as many casualties as a serious attack would demand—and once again there was nothing to show for our pains.

The new sector had been badly knocked about by the enemy bombardment in the attack of the previous week, the breast-works were in a very bad condition, communication trenches had ceased to exist, while there was grave danger of being cut off from the rear, as it took no less than two R.E. companies all their time to keep the three bridges in repair. There was practically no protection from shell-fire, and it was obvious that we were in for a very bad time if the enemy renewed his bombardment. For the first twenty-four hours the Boche was fairly quiet, but at 2-30 a.m. on July 19th he barraged our line very heavily in connection with a raid on the battalion on our left, killing 2nd Lieutenant Bridger and twelve men, and wounding twenty in this bombardment. We were heavily shelled at intervals by day and night for the next day or two, but the fire was, fortunately, inaccurate, and we lost only four men wounded. One trench was constantly shelled by the Boche, with the result that no one lingered there. With their usual genius for nick-names, our men at once christened this "Tout de Suite Alley."

On July 21st a few more men were wounded, and during the night the enemy bombarded Nieuport with shells containing a new kind of gas, now known to all the world as "mustard" gas on account of the peculiar smell and the colour which it stained everything with which it came into contact. It was rarely fatal, but it caused several cases of temporary blindness. The gas was felt at Battalion Headquarters, but the companies in the front line escaped any ill-effects. We were to have been relieved by the 4th K.O.Y.L.I. on the 22nd, but they were unable to get up to us because of the gas. At 11 p.m. that night the enemy barraged us very severely for an hour, and again from 3 a.m. to 4 a.m. on the 23rd. The shelling was heaviest on the support company and on Battalion Headquarters, and we lost thirteen men killed and fifty-nine wounded or gassed. Among the officers, Major Stickney and 2nd Lieutenants Reynolds, Harrison and Ackernley were gassed, while 2nd Lieutenant Beckett was killed by a shell. The latter had been with us for only a few weeks, and this was his first experience of the line.

1917. July—September.

On July 24th the Battalion should have been relieved, this time by the 2/6th Manchesters, but the enemy shelled Nieuport very heavily and demolished the bridges, and again the relief had to be postponed. However, the Manchesters got up to us next day, and by 12 noon the relief was complete. 2nd Lieutenant H. R. Dixon was sent down gassed on the day of relief, and Lieutenant D. P. Grant on the 27th—the latter being succeeded as Adjutant by Captain R. E. Wilson, M.C.

Rumour now said that the Division was to go into the line again at once for an attack, and on the 27th and 28th we practised on trenches dug to represent the enemy lines in the Lombartzyde sector. At 3-30 a.m. on the 29th a dress rehearsal took place. This was carried out satisfactorily, except that a very large amount of coughing, due to gas poisoning, would certainly have given the enemy warning. Fortunately, the Corps Staff who were present realised this, and on the next day we heard that the Division would not be called upon to carry out the attack. Most of the Battalion were feeling the effects of the gas in some degree, and during the week ending July 31st about a hundred men had to be sent into hospital. The last two weeks of July had cost us eight officers and two hundred and eighty other ranks, of whom about half were gas cases. We were still, however, about eight hundred strong, as we had received drafts of some one hundred and seventy men, most of whom were of about four months' service. These included some forty men compulsorily transferred from the A.S.C.

* * * * * *

August and September were in some respects a real summer holiday. Except in case of alarm, the coast defence work at Bray Dunes, Zuydcoote and Fort des Dunes meant a few guards over strong points and ammunition dumps, and training. The Battalion was still suffering from the insidious effects of the gas and from the physical and moral strain of the eight days at Nieuport. The programme of training was therefore compiled with the idea of getting the men fit as quickly as possible. The area between Dunkerque and the front was crowded with troops and transport, and the enemy acknowledged the fact by sending his bombing 'planes over every night. Fortunately, most of the eggs were laid in the vicinity of Dunkerque, but occasionally they fell near enough to disturb our slumbers. Company training, though warm and irksome at times, was pleasant enough on the whole. The sea bathing at Bray Dunes was delightful, and the men played football every evening in spite of the heat.

In the meantime, A Company and half of C Company were sent back to Nieuport on August 10th to work for the 257th Tunnelling Company, R.E. These unfortunate fellows had to work there for eight days while the rest of the Battalion drilled, sweated and bathed at Bray Dunes. On the 18th, however, the Battalion moved forward to Oost Dunkerque, whence B, D and the other half of C Companies were sent to relieve the party at Nieuport. The latter had experienced a lot of Boche hate, and had lost twenty-six men in the eight days—mostly through gas, which remained in the tunnels and cellars for a long time after the shelling had ceased. The second party fared no better, and during the five days, August 18th to 22nd, they sent down fifty-four men gassed. They were relieved on the 23rd by A Company, half of C Company, and a platoon made up from Battalion Headquarters details, who carried on until the 27th, when the whole Battalion marched to Fort des Dunes.

From September 3rd we were in comfortable billets at Bray Dunes in Army Reserve, and could therefore devote ourselves entirely to training and enjoyment. The delights of being at the sea-side in glorious summer weather made up for the long hours of training. There were a number of civilians in the village and a few good shops where the men could buy almost anything from a bathing dress to a tin whistle. An enterprising Belgian photographer did a roaring trade by making atrocious pictures of the men in the attitudes beloved by "Tommy." Football matches were played every day, and it was sometimes possible to go into Dunkerque. There was an excellent range, and the men were able to get much badly-needed practice in shooting, while in the course of several Brigade attack practices we were gratified to see that we had once more made a well-trained battalion out of the mixed drafts of the A.S.C. "comb-outs," etc., which had recently joined. In the Brigade Competitions No. 9 Platoon won the Platoon Drill, and No. 16 the Musketry.

Rumour was very busy among the men at this time, principally because there were now forty officers on the strength. Moreover, a good deal had been heard of "round-topped ridges" in the course of the Brigade attack practices, but it was left to General Godley, Commanding the XXII. Corps, to enlighten us as to what was in store for us. He saw us practice the attack, and afterwards called the officers of the Brigade together to tell us that we were to attack at Passchendaele in the near future.

General Plumer found time to inspect us once again whilst at work on September 11th, and we very much appreciated the fact that he rode round our training ground and saw the Battalion at work, instead of making us stand at attention for hours at a ceremonial Battalion parade.

The Battalion marched away from Bray Dunes to the village of Petit Synthe (about four kilometres west of Dunkerque) on September 22nd. Here all were comfortably billeted. The obnoxious habits of the Hun overhead did not disturb our sleep very much, and we spent the next day doing nothing, as elegantly as we could. Many escaped to Dunkerque and spent an enjoyable day (and much money) there, returning to Petit Synthe in time to miss the evening bomb-dropping.

Movements by 'bus were frequently fine examples of bad organisation, and our move to Wulverdinghe on September 24th was no exception. We paraded at 7-30 a.m., but the lorries did not arrive until 10, and it was nearly noon when the start was made. The debussing point (Lederzeele) was reached at 4 p.m., and the Battalion marched thence to Wulverdinghe, a very pretty village about 10 kilometres north of St. Omer, and thence, three days later, to the villages of Moringhem, Petit Difques and Grand Difques, where we were billeted. The 29th was spent on a capital range firing from dawn to dusk, and on the 30th we took part in a Divisional attack scheme on ground near Quelmes.

On October 1st we marched a further eight kilometres to Salperwick, and early next morning set off to the Nieppe area. We arrived in the afternoon after a march of twenty kilometres, and were billeted in and around a large farm—two companies in barns and two in tents. There was a further march of twenty-three kilometres next day to Watou, where we were given a few tents and a number of tarpaulins and told to make ourselves as comfortable as possible.

* * * * * *

A few personal notes must bring this chapter to an end. On September 14th the Military Medal was awarded to Private W. E. Marshall, of A Company, for gallantry at Nieuport on August 26th, when he rescued a man, under heavy shell fire, from a dug-out which had been blown in.

At Oost Dunkerque, on the 29th August, Captain A. M. B. Firth, who had been shepherding the gentle Hun prisoners for the past two years, returned to us; while 2nd Lieutenant S. E. Warburton, M.M., joined the Battalion at Moringhem. He was one of our old C Company N.C.O.'s, and we were very glad to welcome him back as an officer.

On September 10th, to the great regret of officers and men alike, our padre, the Reverend H. F. Elgood, M.C., left us to be attached to the gunners. He became Senior Chaplain of the Division soon afterwards.

CHAPTER X

THE THIRD BATTLE OF YPRES

(See Map 1)

TO appreciate the Hallamshires' lot in the third Battle of Ypres, a good deal of detailed background must first be examined. By the end of April, 1917, the Arras Battle had resulted in the capture of nearly 20,000 prisoners and immense quantities of materials, while "a great improvement had been effected in the general situation of our troops on the front attacked, and the capture of the Vimy Ridge had removed a constant menace to the security of our line." (1)

In June the Messines-Wytschaete Ridge had been captured. "By this operation the Second Army front was pushed forward as far as was then desirable," and "it became possible to take in hand our final dispositions for our main offensive east and north of Ypres." (1)

It was impossible to follow up immediately the successes of the first day of the battle(2), because, "during the afternoon, while fighting was still in progress, rain began, and fell steadily all night. Thereafter, for four days, the rain continued without cessation, and for several days afterwards the weather remained stormy and unsettled. The low-lying, clayey soil, torn by shells and sodden with rain, turned to a succession of vast muddy pools. The valleys of the choked and overflowing streams were speedily transformed into long stretches of bog, impassable except by a few well-defined tracks, which became marks for the enemy's artillery. To leave these tracks was to risk death by drowning, and in the course of the subsequent fighting on several occasions both men and pack animals were lost in this way. In these conditions operations of any magnitude became impossible, and the resumption of our offensive was necessarily postponed until a period of fine weather should allow the ground to recover.

"As had been the case in the Arras battle, this unavoidable delay in the development of our offensive was of the greatest service

(1) Sir D. Haig's Despatch, 25/12/1917.
(2) 31st July, 1917.

1917. OCTOBER.

to the enemy. Valuable time was lost, the troops opposed to us were able to recover from the disorganisation produced by our first attack, and the enemy was given the opportunity to bring up reinforcements." (1)

Fighting had been continued in the latter part of August and throughout September; while the success of the attack on October 3-4 "marked a definite step in the development of our advance. Our line had now been established along the main ridge for 9,000 yards from our starting point near Mount Sorrel. From the furthest point reached the well-marked Gravenstafel Spur offered a defensible feature along which our line could be bent back from the ridge.

"The year was far spent. The weather had been consistently unpropitious, and the state of the ground, in consequence of rain and shelling combined, made movement inconceivably difficult. The resultant delays had given the enemy time to bring up reinforcements and to organise his defence after each defeat. Even so, it was still the difficulty of movement far more than hostile resistance which continued to limit our progress, and now made it doubtful whether the capture of the remainder of the ridge before winter finally set in was possible.

"On the other hand, there was no reason to anticipate an abnormally wet October. The enemy had suffered severely, as was evidenced by the number of prisoners in our hands, by the number of his dead on the battlefield, by the costly failure of his repeated counter-attacks, and by the symptoms of confusion and discouragement in his ranks.

"In this connection, documents captured in the course of the battle of the 4th October throw an interesting light upon the success of the measures taken by us to meet the enemy's new system of defence by counter-attacks. These documents show that the German Higher Command had already recognised the failure of their methods, and were endeavouring to revert to something approximating to their old practice of holding their forward positions in strength.

"After weighing these considerations, as well as the general situation and various other factors affecting the problem, among them the desirability of assisting our Allies in the operations to be carried out by them on the 23rd October in the neighbourhood of Malmaison, I decided to continue the offensive further and to renew the advance at the earliest possible moment consistent with adequate preparation.

(1) Sir D. Haig's Despatch, 25/12/1917.

1917. OCTOBER.

"Accordingly, I determined to deliver the next combined French and British attack on the 9th October. . . . Unfortunately, bad weather still persisted in the early part of October, and on the 7th October heavy rain fell all day. The unfavourable conditions interfered with our artillery preparation; but every effort was made to engage the enemy's batteries in their new positions, and on the date last mentioned our artillery co-operated effectively in the repulse of two hostile attacks.

"On the 8th October rain continued, and the slippery state of the ground, combined with an exceptionally dark night, made the assembling of troops a matter of considerable difficulty. No interference, however, was encountered from the enemy's artillery, and at 5-20 a.m. on the 9th October our attack was renewed on a front of over six miles, from a point east of Zonnebeke to our junction with the French north-west of Langemarck. On our left our Allies prolonged the front of attack to a point opposite Draaibank. At the same time, minor operations were undertaken on the right of our main attack, east and south-east of Polygon Wood.

"The greatest depth of our advance was on the left, where the Allied troops penetrated the German positions to a distance of nearly one and a half miles. . . . . . Early in the afternoon both French and British troops had established themselves on their final objectives on the outskirts of Houthulst Forest.

"On the right of the Guards, other English Divisions made equal progress along the Ypres-Staden Railway. . . . . .

"Further south, English battalions fought their way forward in the face of great opposition to the eastern outskirts of Poelcappelle village. *Australian troops and East Lancashire, Yorkshire and South Midland Territorials carried our line forward in the direction of Passchendaele and up the western slopes of the main ridge, capturing Nieuwemolen and Keerselaarhoek and a number of strong points and fortified farms."* (1)

This account, while dismissing our part of the battle in some three or four lines, shows clearly the extraordinarily adverse conditions under which it was played. Once again our men behaved splendidly, but had no great chance.

In preparation for the battle the Battalion had been reduced to battle strength by October 5th. Major Welsh (now second-in-command), Captains Holmes and Brooke, 2nd Lieutenants Williams,

(1) Sir D. Haig's Despatch, 25/12/1917.

Payne and Rimer, and 60 O.R.'s, were sent to the Anzac Corps Reinforcement Camp near Hazebrouck, while about a dozen men were lent to the Divisional M.G. Company to act as carriers in the battle. Meanwhile, the Medical Officer (Captain Smythe) went into hospital and was replaced by Captain W. J. Allen.

The three days spent in the field near Watou were full of discomfort. The tents and tarpaulins were old and leaky and not sufficient to accommodate the Battalion without great overcrowding. The whole Battalion was pleased to pack up its traps on October 6th and proceed by lorry to Vlamertinghe.

We embussed at Watou at about 5 p.m., but did not start away until two hours later. The journey took three hours—although the distance was only fifteen kilometres—on account of the congestion of traffic on the roads. The night was pitch dark, and no vehicles were allowed to carry lights. The main road from Poperinghe to Ypres was packed with an endless stream of motor lorries, heavy guns hauled by caterpillar tractors, parties of troops on foot, and countless G.S. wagons and limbers. Vlamertinghe was a very badly-wrecked village—every house was more or less smashed—but we made ourselves as comfortable as possible in what was left of the cellars and basements. After our three days under the leaky tarpaulin, the billets in "Vlam" were comparatively palatial, but we had no blankets, and it was very cold at night. To add to our discomfort, the Boche gave us a violent bombing from 2 a.m. to 3 a.m., though beyond disturbing our sleep, no harm was done. Next day, October 7th, the C.O. went up to reconnoitre the front in the sector where we were due to attack on the 9th. Everyone was busily engaged in making preparations for the battle. Each company sent one officer and ten O.R.'s forward to reconnoitre generally and to learn the way up to the front, so that they could lead the Battalion when required. These parties received no further instructions, and it was not altogether surprising that, in the turmoil of the Ypres Salient, they got completely lost. They were unable to find the Battalion in time to take any part in the battle, and were a distinct loss to our fighting strength.

During the afternoon A Company, together with one officer and four N.C.O.'s from each other company, were sent forward to Potijze—which had once been a village, but had been shelled out of existence—where the remainder of the Battalion were to follow next day.

The C.O. returned from his reconnaissance with only very

1917. OCTOBER.

scanty verbal instructions about the fight, and it was not until 3 a.m. next morning that the Brigade Operation Orders were received. These orders were at once sent round to the companies, and the men's packs and great-coats collected and dumped in the village. At 6 a.m. the Battalion marched away to the muddy fields of Potijze and Wieltje. Here the day was spent in drawing and issuing extra S.A.A., grenades, sandbags, etc., and in doing the hundred and one things necessary before an attack. Officers were dressed in the ordinary S.D. jacket, trousers and puttees exactly like the men, except that they wore their badges of rank on the shoulder straps and a two-inch square of white cloth sewn on to the back of the jacket to enable our men to recognise them easily.

During the day, October 8th, the rain fell heavily and ceaselessly, and the ground and tracks were in an indescribably muddy state. 2nd Lieutenant Jackson(1) and the Battalion Scouts went forward to reconnoitre and tape out the assembly position early in the afternoon, and at 4-45 p.m. the Battalion marched forward once more. Each man, in addition to carrying a full water bottle, had been provided with a bottle full of tea mixed with a small ration of rum, and this proved of incalculable value. The distance from Potijze to the assembly position was not more than seven kilometres, as the crow flies, but by the winding tracks it was probably twelve. The tracks all ran across ground which had been won from the enemy within the last two months, and had been subjected to very intense shell fire—and the rain fell pitilessly the whole time. Through batteries of guns, past heaps of unburied dead Germans, into a very inferno of confusion and noise, the Battalion advanced to the position of assembly. The terrible conditions of the march can perhaps be realised, to some extent, when it is stated that we did not reach our position until 4 a.m.—*i.e.,* one hour and twenty minutes before zero hour. Our men had been marching for eleven and a quarter hours, and were soaked with rain and nearly exhausted.

The Brigade attacked with the 5th Y. and L. on the left, the Hallamshires on the right, the 5th K.O.Y.L.I. supporting the 5th Y. and L., and the 4th K.O.Y.L.I. in reserve. The West Yorkshire Brigade attacked on the left; 66th Division troops on the right.

At 5-20 a.m. the barrage opened and the Battalion went forward to the attack. The Ravebeek stream was the first serious obstacle

(1) 2nd Lieutenant Jackson was now acting as Scout Officer, vice Lieutenant Gifford, promoted to the position of Brigade Intelligence Officer.

1917. OCTOBER.

encountered. This stream, flowing diagonally across the line of attack, was considerably swollen after the rains, and for about fifty yards on either side of it the ground was much cut up and very wet. In many places the water was waist deep.

A Company (Captain T. G. Sorby) and C Company (Captain J. F. Wortley) led, C being on the right. C Company at once came under an annihilating machine-gun fire, and only about fifty men succeeded in crossing the stream; the remainder continued to advance up the left bank. B Company (Captain P. N. Johnson, M.C.), who were to "leap-frog" through C to take the second objective, came under very heavy machine-gun fire from Waterfields and Laamkeek, and were unable to reach the stream. On the left, the machine-gun fire was not so heavy, and A Company, crossing the stream by the Gravenstafel road, fought its way almost to its objective and consolidated. D Company (Lieutenant T. A. Merry) attempted to "leap-frog" through A, but were pinned down by machine-gun fire. Meanwhile, the party of C Company, which had crossed the stream, had been reduced to about ten men, and they, helped by a few stragglers from the 66th Division, formed a thin line of posts between A Company's right and the marsh.

Our barrage was very unsatisfactory. The enemy machine-gunners should have been knocked out, or at least badly shaken by a good barrage on them and their pill-boxes. As it was, the barrage was very weak and so ragged that it was difficult to tell the line of it. This weakness was not due to any lack of energy or skill on the part of the gunners, but to the abominable weather and the bottomless mud. On the 4th—the last day of fine weather—an advance of about a mile had been made, but the gunners had been quite unable to bring forward their guns afterwards. Many had been knocked out by enemy fire, others had sunk into the mud, and the few that could fire were loosing off at almost extreme range. The inevitable result was a weak and inaccurate barrage. Not a single Boche was found killed by shell fire, although we found many killed and wounded by our rifles and Lewis guns.

Further progress being impossible, the Battalion consolidated on the line taken up by A and C Companies, about 700 or 800 yards from the tape line. The C.O. established his Headquarters immediately in rear of this line near the remains of a farm appropriately known as "Marsh Bottom," and there the Battalion stayed in the water-logged shell-holes until 10-30 p.m. on the night of October 10th.

1917. OCTOBER.

The enemy troops were of a Jäger Regiment, and were remarkably good snipers. We suffered many casualties at their hands during those two days, particularly among our stretcher-bearers and runners, while many wounded men were hit as they attempted to crawl to the rear.

At about 5 p.m. on the 9th we saw two hundred of the enemy forming up for a counter-attack on our left company. We put up the S.O.S. and opened rifle and Lewis-gun fire on them, with the result that the counter-attack did not develop. At about 4-15 a.m. next day the C.O. received information that our airmen had reported the presence of British troops in the vicinity of Snipe Hall (a ruined farm, plus concrete pill-box, 450 yards in front of our position). He was instructed to "mop up" the ground up to Snipe Hall, to assist in which operation a barrage was to be put down at 4-45 a.m. The notice given was so short that it was impossible to organise this attack, but strong patrols were sent forward, and, although they obtained contact with the enemy, they could find no trace of British troops.

During the whole day and night the enemy kept up a heavy artillery fire, but most of his shells fell behind our position into the Ravebeek valley and on the Gravenstafel ridge. The enemy fire was chiefly high explosive, but there were gas shells at intervals, especially at night time. Our officers and men did very good work throughout the day in keeping down the sniping of the enemy, Lieutenant Merry, in particular, being credited with a very fine bag. During the night, 9/10th October, the Jäger troops were relieved, and next day the enemy sniping was not so effective.

How Lieutenant Philip Branson and his transport men were able to bring up rations and stores through the mud and shell-fire is a mystery. It seemed perfectly impossible that they could survive the shelling even if the ground had not been so awful, yet, in the fading light of each afternoon, these gallant men—and gallant mules—were streaming over the ridges towards the front line.

At 10-30 p.m. on the 10th the Hallamshires were relieved by a battalion of New Zealanders and marched to a bivouac camp about a mile east of Vlamertinghe. Every man was suffering more or less from trench feet, for we had been lying in water-logged shell-holes for nearly two days. The camp was not reached until 5 a.m., and five hours later we marched off again to Ypres, entraining there for Hopoutre. We had a ten-mile march thence to a camp near Winnizeele, and on arrival at about 5 p.m. tents were rapidly allotted and everyone at once went off into the sleep of utter exhaustion.

1917. OCTOBER.

Casualties in the forty-eight hours amounted to ten officers—Lieutenant Poole and 2nd Lieutenants Jackson, Benyon and de Bell killed; 2nd Lieutenant B. O. Robinson missing; and Captain Sorby, Lieutenants Bagshaw, Cloud and Gladwin, and 2nd Lieutenant Burwell wounded. Of other ranks, forty-two were killed, forty-eight missing, and one hundred and ten wounded.

Among the many gallant deeds done on October 9th not the least was that which won Captain Francis Wortley his M.C. The official account read as follows:—

"This officer was in command of a company which had to cross a marsh in front of the first objective. He succeeded in doing this by wading waist deep under heavy M.G. and rifle fire. With ten men he attempted most gallantly to reach a pill-box near which a large number of the enemy were firing at him. When only he and his runner were left he sniped eight of the enemy, and then, finding that no reinforcements were arriving, withdrew, re-organised what was left of his company, and proceeded to consolidate the ground gained."

In addition to this award, the D.C.M. was given to C.S.M. W. Wagg, and the M.M. to Privates R. Mackie, J. W. Wilson, P. Jenkinson, F. Lockwood, Sergeants J. E. Warren and L. Lawless, Private G. Downes, Sergeant R. Megson, Corporal H. Green and Lance-Corporal E. Bower.

It only remains to add the following extract from Sir Douglas Haig's despatch, 25th December, 1917:—

"Throughout the northern operations our troops have been fighting over ground every foot of which is sacred to the memory of those who, in the first and second battles of Ypres, fought and died to make possible the victories of the armies which to-day are rolling back the tide stayed by their sacrifice. It is no disparagement of the gallant deeds performed on other fronts to say that, in the stubborn struggle for the line of hills which stretches from Wytschaete to Passchendaele, the great armies that to-day are shouldering the burden of our Empire have shown themselves worthy of the regiments which, in October and November of 1914, made Ypres take rank for ever amongst the most glorious of British battles.

"Throughout the months of strenuous fighting which have wiped the old Ypres salient from the battle map of Flanders, the finest qualities of our infantry have been displayed. The great material disadvantages of the position from which they had to attack, the strength of the enemy's fortifications, and the extraordinary hard-

1917. OCTOBER.

ships imposed by the conditions of ground and weather during August and throughout the later stages of the attack, called for the exercise of courage, determination and endurance to a degree which has never been surpassed in war."

CHAPTER XI

THE WINTER, 1917-18.

(See Map 1)

(a) After Passchendaele.

THE weary battle for Passchendaele Ridge was continued throughout October. Division after division was flung into the cauldron of fire and mud with varying success. Sometimes an advance of a few hundred yards was made, sometimes the attacks failed completely, but there was always the same tale of heavy casualties. East of Ypres the whole salient was one vast sea of mud strewn with the wreckage of war. There was not a sign of vegetation anywhere; scarcely a brick remained of the farms with which the area had been dotted; nothing could be seen for miles but men and horses (alive or dead), guns, débris and MUD.

On entering the salient, one kept to the "roads." It was hardly possible to tell that there were roads—they could only be distinguished by the feel of something solid beneath the top layer of slimy mud. Further on the roads disappeared altogether, and duck-board tracks became the only routes across the bog. In the actual area of the front line, there were not even duck-boards; and men were here floundering and sinking, swearing and kicking, wrenching themselves free and shooting—and being shot—and the man who fell wounded and unseen in that all-devouring mud had a mighty poor chance. The surface of the mud was littered with the débris of the fighting. Derelict tanks by the score could be seen half-sunken in the mud, where they had been pounded to pieces by the Boche gunners. The bodies of horses and mules lay around in every direction—many of the animals shot by their own drivers because they had become hopelessly stuck in the mud. Guns of every calibre and description were lined up wheel to wheel and were firing almost continuously night and day. When they fired a barrage at night thousands of red angry flames shot out of the muzzles in such rapid succession that, from the front line, the gun area appeared as a blaze of light. The enemy usually replied vigorously to these barrages, and to the infantrymen beneath it seemed impossible that so many thousands of shells could be passing through the air simultaneously in opposite directions without meeting!

Slow as was the infantry advance in this battle, the guns found it well nigh impossible to keep pace with them. Horses were pitifully useless to pull the guns in the mud, and most of them were man-handled forward. Many guns became hopelessly stuck, and had to be abandoned to sink gradually into the slime. Under these awful conditions, from July 31st to November 6th, the British attacks continued—but the worst month of all was October. Our own attack was not a failure, as we had advanced our line some 700 yards—but at a cost of one man per ten feet.

Major-General E. M. Perceval, who had been in command of the Division for two and a quarter years, retired to England after the battle, and our Brigade Commander, Brigadier-General R. L. Adlercron, was similarly transferred. These officers were succeeded by Major-General N. J. G. Cameron and Brigadier-General L. F. Green-Wilkinson respectively, both of whom remained with us until the end of the war.

On October 15th the Hallamshires paraded once more facing east, but before starting off there was a diversion in the shape of a fire. We had been shivering in the open for the past fortnight, and were therefore not altogether sorry to find a huge barn well ablaze in our midst. By the time the blaze was got in hand, all were comfortably warm; and although the farmer claimed some forty thousand francs, we were inclined to think it was worth the money. The shoe-makers, who had been living in the barn, vehemently denied any culpability in the matter, so, unless the fire was caused by the rats, it must remain one of the unsolved mysteries of the Great War.

At 7 a.m. we were packed into motor lorries and hustled off to Ypres, debussing at the Menin Gate and marching to our camp at Potijze. About a dozen tents and several old tarpaulins were provided, but by "scrounging" in the neighbourhood we obtained enough old sheets of corrugated iron and timber to make ourselves passably comfortable. The camp was on high ground, which was exposed to the full force of the biting winds, and we suffered considerably from the cold. On account of enemy aircraft, no lights or fires were allowed after dusk, and for the same reason tents were struck before dawn. The Boche shelled us throughout the day in a desultory fashion, so that orders (received on the 18th) to go up to the front line were not altogether unwelcome.

1917. OCTOBER.

At 11 o'clock that morning everything was packed up ready for the march off at noon, and the men were lying about smoking or writing letters, when, without the slightest warning, a number of bombs fell among us from two enemy aeroplanes flying very high. In a few seconds fifty men were killed and wounded, and many others had miraculous escapes. No officer was hit, but Major Welsh was so shaken up that he went to hospital and never returned to us. Captain Holmes, the senior company commander, was ordered to report to Battalion Headquarters to act as Second-in-Command, and the command of A Company devolved upon Lieutenant F. J. Wilkins. 2nd Lieutenant W. Ryan was appointed Scout Officer, vice 2nd Lieutenant Jackson, who had been killed on the 9th.

At 12-15 p.m. we marched away by platoons to the line—an exciting move, as the Boche was shelling the road heavily. The day had turned out very fine and clear, and enemy observation balloons were out in full force. By the time the Battalion had reached the vicinity of Zonnebeke it was obvious that the enemy had seen the long column of troops (the whole Brigade was on the road), and the shelling became more intense. It was 2 p.m. by the time we reached Hill 40 (about two thousand yards from the line), and as the relief was not due to commence until 4 p.m. and the enemy had put down a veritable barrage in front and to the right of us, the C.O. decided to deploy the Battalion on the hill. The leading platoons, therefore, were sent off to fill a line of shell-holes near the top, and eventually the whole Brigade was deployed into lines of platoons. For the next hour or more the enemy kept up a steady fire, but the majority of the shells fell about 150 yards to our right in the vicinity of what had once been Zonnebeke Station. The air was thick with flying splinters of shell, but the only casualty was a briar pipe which was suddenly removed from its owner's mouth by a lump of shell.

By 6-20 p.m. the relief was complete, the Hallamshires taking over the front line, which was merely a series of shell holes, from the 34th and part of the 36th Battalions Australian Infantry. Battalion Headquarters were at Boethoek, an unpleasant pill-box with a ceiling about four feet high. A, B and D Companies in the front line had a joint headquarters at Hamburg House, a pill-box built at a road junction. Probably because of its position, this pill-box was shelled heavily and accurately, but was very strongly built and survived several direct hits.

The whole of the area was still in a terrible state—black slime

1917. OCTOBER.

littered with dead bodies, weapons and equipment of every kind. The Engineers were kept hard at it laying duck-board tracks, and much of the Boche equipment was salved and sent down later on.

The transport, animals and personnel, had to undergo many hardships, and it was often due solely to the perseverance and grit of our transport men that we got our rations at all. They were invariably shelled on the journey to and from the line, and the nights brought the regular visits of the Boche bombers, who appeared to make a special target of horse lines.

Our fellows settled down into their positions in (or, rather, on) the front line and at once began to make bits of trench out of shell-holes and to dig "cubby-holes" to give themselves a little protection from the weather at least. The cheerful *sang-froid* of the men and their courage and endurance, under the most depressing conditions of ground and weather, were the admiration of every officer in the Battalion.

In the early morning of October 19th the enemy shelled our area with "tear" gas, but although it made everybody sneeze violently, it produced no harmful results, and this was followed up by an intense counter-preparation barrage, to which our guns replied vigorously. This heavy shelling continued for more than an hour, and was repeated for shorter periods at intervals throughout the day.

We were again heavily shelled in the afternoon of the 20th, and it was noticeable that the shells were all 10 cm. or larger. The ubiquitous 77 mm. shell was conspicuous by its absence, and this pointed to the fact that the enemy expected further attacks, and had withdrawn his light guns. At this time we were frequently shelled by the enemy with British shells fired from British 6-inch howitzers which had been captured from the Russians.

On October 21st (a Sunday) we were given an extra large dose of Boche hate, and at 5-35 a.m. on Monday our guns put down a real attack barrage, although there was no attack taking place. The Hun got thoroughly windy, put up his S.O.S., and replied with a fierce barrage on our lines, but the enemy fire soon died down when he found that the British were not coming over to breakfast after all. The Staff frequently sent out details of such shoots as this too late to give warning to patrols before the barrage came down. On this occasion we had a patrol out in Augustus Wood when the barrage opened—the enemy counter-barrage fell heavily on to the Wood (probably his S.O.S. lines)—and the patrol escaped by a miracle. In the evening of the 22nd the 50th Canadians relieved us, and after being shelled all the way down the tracks (particularly "K" track) we reached the old bivouacs of Potijze, and on the following day moved back by bus to a camp near Winnezeele.

Meanwhile, the transport lines had been roughly handled by the Boche heavies, but in spite of the loss of 30 animals, the T.O. managed to move all his wagons to Winnezeele on the 23rd.

There was a further march to billets near Steenvoorde on October 27th. The Battalion was scattered over rather a wide area, but everybody was very thankful to see the last of the leaky tents. The weather was getting very cold and fuel was very scarce—so scarce that one mess had to burn their gramophone records to keep warm! The Battalion stayed in these billets for fifteen days, during which time several training schemes were carried out, and there were several short route marches.

(b) The Salient Again.

On November 11th we marched a few kilometres to a field just over the frontier into Belgium, and were thence sent on to Walker Camp, near Dickebusch. Here the Battalion was housed in waterproof huts fitted with stoves—the most comfortable billets we had occupied for some time, in spite of the enemy's disturbing habit of shelling the camp with high velocity shells occasionally.

On the 24th the Battalion marched forward to Ypres and was billeted in the Ramparts, the tunnels of which, though undesirable as residences, were at least good cover from shell fire. Some of the officers explored the ruined houses in the vicinity and found quite good rooms for billets.

Three days later a further move forward was made to the front line area, the Battalion marching *via* Derby Road—Shrapnel Corner—Warrington Road—Birr X Roads—Helles Track and Jabber Track. The companies were echeloned on the Tokio and Westhoek Ridges, all of which were shelled ceaselessly by the enemy. The tracks were given particular attention, especially at night time.

Our rations were brought up to Battalion Headquarters at Garter Point, an old pill-box in the valley between Tokio and Anzac Ridges. No one envied the transport men their nightly journey up those shell-swept tracks, nor did the companies enjoy the journey to Battalion Headquarters to fetch their allotted number of sand-bags filled with bread, meat, jam, etc.

1917. NOVEMBER—DECEMBER.

The scarcity of water was a great difficulty. Every drop had to be brought up by the ration mules in petrol tins, of which there must have been tens of thousands in the Salient. This water was, of course, only used for cooking and drinking, and there was seldom even a cupful to spare for washing. The water in the shell-holes could not be used for ablution purposes, as it was contaminated by gas and other things.

On December 1st we moved forward—A, B and C Companies to the front line, with D Company in support. Battalion Headquarters was in a pill-box at Molenaarelsthoek, nicknamed "Molly's Nook." The front line now consisted of a series of short lengths of trench, constructed from linked-up shell-holes. It was not possible to do any cooking, and all rations were sent up ready cooked. Every night we worked on the trenches, improving and extending them and putting out more wire in front. During the day we got what rest we could, as movement always brought fire upon us. Most of the enemy shelling was from 15 cm. guns, and a large proportion of it fell on and about the ridges behind us, the front line itself being comparatively quiet. Patrolling was vigorously carried out every night in front of the Battalion.

The Corps Summary of Intelligence (better known as "Comic Cuts") had reported a Boche machine gun at a point north of Celtic Wood. Our Scouts were ordered to confirm the presence of this gun. They advanced very warily towards the position, and to their surprise (for these things usually were NOT there), they could see the gun on a slight mound in the faint moonlight—but could see or hear nothing of the enemy gunners. Careful manœuvring at last brought them within a few yards of the gun. They made a dash forward, seized the gun, and—turned the handle! It was an antediluvian cattle-cake-breaking machine!

On the morning of December 4th 2nd Lieutenant Gadsby took out a patrol in the direction of Justice Wood and ran into the arms of a large party of the enemy. Our men made a fighting retirement, but lost two men killed, two missing and one wounded.

The Battalion was relieved at 6 p.m. on December 5th. It was pitch dark at that hour, and it was difficult to keep to the narrow duck-board tracks, while eight men were wounded by shell-fire on the way out. On arrival at Ypres, where we were billeted for the night, hot food awaited us, and our cellar holes in the Ramparts had quite an attractive appearance. One felt on these occasions that it was almost

1917. DECEMBER.

worth while going into the line if only for the pleasure of coming out! Next morning the Battalion marched away to Vancouver Camp, near Vlamertinghe, where it stayed for five days with no worries beyond a little drill by day and a little bombing by night. Lieutenant Grant rejoined on December 7th, and resumed his duties as Adjutant, Captain Wilson taking over the command of B Company.

The Battalion marched to Vlamertinghe next morning and there entrained in the usual cattle trucks and proceeded very slowly to Ypres, detraining in a field near the School. At this point we proposed to eat our dinner, but the Boche began to shell the field, and we moved up the railway cutting to Hellfire Corner, dumping ourselves in a field north of the Menin Road. The meal completed, at 3 p.m. we began the trek up that terribly long duck-board track, which was known as "Mole Track." Four hours of walking brought us to our position in the line on the Broodseinde Ridge. Battalion Headquarters were again at "Molly's Nook."

During our second night in the line the sentries of a post on the right (B Company) sector saw some men approaching their post. The sentries waited until the men got close up to them, and then challenged. The reply was a guttural Boche exclamation, so the sentries opened fire on them and then ordered the Boche to come in and surrender. The enemy, apparently, understood the order, for four at once gave themselves up, and of the remaining two, one was lying dead and the other escaped, wounded. These prisoners declared that they were a party sent to carry rations, and that they had lost their way. They were wearing patrol equipment and carried rifles and hand bayonets, so that the ration-carrier yarn required some swallowing. The sentries (Privates C. Dungworth and V. Rogers) were awarded the Military Medal, and Captain Wilson received the General's congratulations on the vigilance of his sentries.

Jabber Track was becoming increasingly unhealthy, as the enemy appeared to have taken a sudden dislike to it and shelled it violently at intervals. On December 13th, for instance—chiefly owing to this unpleasantness—we had one man killed, and 2nd Lieutenant Kirby (who had only just joined us) and twelve men were wounded.

We constructed an excellent observation post inside a wrecked pill-box on the crest of Broodseinde Ridge. From this a constant watch was kept, but there was very little movement to be seen, probably because the enemy held his advance posts at night only.

From December 17th to 23rd the Hallamshires were in support

1917. DECEMBER.

on the ridges, just behind the front. During most of that time our men were employed in putting up wire defences on Broodseinde Ridge, behind the front of the right battalion sector. The weather was bitterly cold and foggy. Work was carried out in the daytime, as it was possible to move quite freely under cover of the mist. The ground was frozen so hard that it was almost impossible to drive the wire pickets into it.

On December 23rd the 5th West Ridings relieved us and we marched out to the Belgian Chateau. In spite of thirteen days in the front line area, the men were remarkably clean and fresh, doubtless because of the fine frosty weather. In the thirteen days four men were killed, and one officer and eighteen men were wounded.(1)

The whole of our Brigade was now out of the line and in Divisional support. Battalion Headquarters were at Belgian Chateau itself, and the companies were billeted near by in Nissen huts. On Chrismas Eve the "Times" informed us that Colonel Branson, Major Stickney, Captain Wortley, Lieutenants Sanderson and Gladwin, and Sergeant Naylor had been mentioned in despatches, and in the New Year's List Colonel Branson received his D.S.O. We supplied working and salvage parties from the 24th to the 28th, but on Christmas Day the work ceased at 11-30 a.m. in order to get the men back to camp in good time for their Christmas Dinner at 2 p.m. As Battalion Headquarters were in the Chateau, the C.O. was able to entertain all the officers to a very jolly dinner—with a splendid programme supplied by Drum-Major Manser, the drums, and a few amateurs! At this Christmas dinner, and at many other times during the war, we were able to appreciate the advantage of having friends at home. A small committee of old officers, consisting of Colonel G. E. Branson, Major W. Tozer, Major J. Wortley, Captain Hay, and others, with Captain S. J. Robinson as Officer i/c Administration, saw to it that many luxuries and minor necessaries not obtainable from Army stores reached us—and we were not ungrateful.

The Battalion marched forward again on December 29th and occupied some new Nissen huts near the ruins of Hussar Farm at Potijze. The camp was not completely ready for occupation, but in the next two days every available man was turned out and the job finished. We also revetted the sides of all the huts as a protection (more or less) against bombing. Parties of men were sent off each day

(1) At this time there were forty-two officers, but only 634 other ranks, on the strength of the Battalion.

1918. January.

to work on Anzac Ridge for the Canadian Tunnellers, and a hundred men worked at making a plank road near Bavaria House. This was the daily programme until January 4th, when we relieved the 5th K.O.Y.L.I. in the left sub-sector of the front. C and D Companies were in the front line, with A in support and B in reserve, Battalion Headquarters being in a tunnel close to Seine X Roads. From here a party went over the ground of our battle in the previous October and secured several identifications of men who had been reported "missing." The site of the battle was now some two thousand yards behind the line, and still bore tragic evidence of the fighting that had taken place there.

Our "front line" in this sector was easier to find on the map than on the ground. It was merely a line of posts, each consisting of a few joined-up shell-holes, with here and there a few yards of proper trench. There were no communication trenches at all, and movement during the day-time was very difficult and was not encouraged by the Boche.

During the six days here we lost only six men wounded. On January 7th snow fell for several hours and added to our discomfort in the line. The enemy was comparatively quiet until January 8th, when the artillery fire increased considerably, and on the 9th he shelled the whole Battalion area heavily from 10 a.m. to 11-30 a.m., and intermittently throughout the day.

(c) St. Marie Cappel.

On January 10th the Division was relieved by the 66th Division, the Hallamshires handing over their part of the line to the 2/5th East Lancs. and marching back to Hussar Camp for the night. Mere holes in the earth—and not the comfortable Nissen huts—were our lot this time, and as the thaw had set in, it was a matter of some difficulty to tuck the men away for the night in the muddy shelters and bivouacs. On the following morning the Battalion marched to a road near Kruisstraat, where scores of motor lorries were drawn up in line. After the regulation wait and a journey of some five hours, we debussed at St. Sylvester Cappel and marched to the next village, St. Marie Cappel, where we were billeted for sixteen days. The men's billets were very good, while those of the officers were positively luxurious compared with any others they had occupied since September. The Battalion was scattered over a large area, but even this had its advantages, at least from a company point of view! The fact that there was very little ground available for training was a distinct drawback, but the local farmers were bribed to let us use some of their fields for drill and football.

The mornings were devoted to training, and a very comprehensive programme was carried out. Every afternoon there were several games of football, and some very good inter-platoon matches were played. Brigadier-General L. F. Green-Wilkinson presented a silver cup for competition by company football teams in the Brigade. Our C Company team was a hot favourite from the start. Led by Captain Wortley, they made short work of our own company teams, afterwards defeating the 5th Y. and L. team, and finally the 4th K.O.Y.L.I. (4-0), thus securing the cup. The village schoolroom was the scene of several evening concerts, no less enjoyable because of the wonderfully stuffy atmosphere, the discomfort of the children's desks, and a glass or two of beer! The Tykes, too, were not far away at this time.

On January 20th we were joined by an officer of the Sherwood Foresters as Second-in-Command of the Battalion. Possibly there were reasons for finding an appointment for an officer of another regiment, but it was felt that we had officers in the Battalion who could have carried a major's crown efficiently.

The Brigadier went on leave to England on January 25th, and Colonel Branson took over command of the Brigade.

(d) The Corps Line.

All good things come to an end, and on January 27th the Battalion marched regretfully from St. Marie Cappel to Caestre, about five kilometres away, where it entrained and was taken to Brandhoek, a village on the main Ypres Road, midway between Poperinghe and Vlamertinghe. We marched thence a further three kilometres to Montreal Camp—a miscellaneous collection of Armstrong and Nissen huts built on the side of the Vlamertinghe—Ouderdom Road.

For the next two weeks seventy-five per cent. of the Battalion made a daily pilgrimage to the front line area for work on a series of strong posts on the forward slopes of Anzac Ridge. These posts were carefully sited and very well designed. They were made complete with dug-out accommodation and wire defences, and they ran in a continuous line down the whole of the Corps front. Although the actual working time was only three hours per day, our four posts were completed in the time allotted. Every morning we turned out of billets at

4-45 a.m. and were taken by lorry to Brandhoek Siding, whence an ancient passenger train carried us some ten kilometres to Hellfire Corner, east of Ypres. By that time we were generally half dead with cold, and were only too glad to get out and march up Cavalry Road, and then for about seven kilometres up Mole Track (or "Never-ending Track," as the men called it) in single file. The journey on the duck-board track alone took about two hours, and the men declared that it was making them web-footed! As we got down from our train on those bitterly cold mornings we little thought that within three months Cavalry Road would be our front line, and Hellfire Corner in "No Man's Land," the ill-fated Corps Line having been abandoned without a shot being fired.

One morning the train started away from Brandhoek Siding as usual, but had not gone more than two or three hundred yards when an ominous grinding noise was heard, and she began to bump and sway violently. The R.O.D. drivers managed to stop her before she turned over, but it was found that the whole of the front part of the train had left the metals and the coaches were leaning over at a most alarming angle. We thought we should certainly have a day's holiday, but the Railway Operating Department sent another train up from Poperinghe in less than a quarter of an hour!

The working parties usually got back to camp at about 2 p.m., by which time they were ravenously hungry, although they always took "haversack rations" with them to the work. The enemy did not interfere with the proceedings, although he was now trying a new and annoying method of shelling. He would concentrate the fire of a number of guns of different calibre upon a given spot and blaze away for a couple of minutes, when the fire would as suddenly cease. However, as the capture of Passchendaele had more or less blinded the enemy in this sector, he did not often do damage to anything but the poor long-suffering earth.

The popular cries of the day were:

"What have YOU salved to-day?"

"Salve more and save shipping."

From Corps Commander to Sanitary Man the salvage fever had got into our blood, and in fourteen days the Battalion salved and brought back from the line goods worth thousands of pounds. Boche machine guns, cartridge belts, shell cases, steel helmets, rifles, bayonets, rum jars, bombs—anything and everything that might conceivably be worth a farthing was carried down those miles of duck-board tracks and into the train, and finally dumped into our limbers at Brandhoek Siding.

While at Montreal Camp the Battalion received drafts to the number of 315 men. Of these, 171 had been transferred from the 2/5th Y. and L. and 100 from the 14th Y. and L., both of which battalions had been disbanded under the new scheme of organisation, which provided for only three battalions per brigade.[1]

On February 6th it was announced that the Belgian Croix de Guerre had been awarded to R.S.M. Imisson and C.S.M. Wood, the veteran Sergeant-Major of B Company.

(e) Moulle.

Entraining at Brandhoek Siding on February 11th, we were taken in the familiar cattle trucks to Watten, near St. Omer, a distance of more than fifty kilometres. We arrived there late at night, and marched a further six kilometres to exceptionally good billets at Moulle. The sole drawback was the fact that the Battalion was scattered over a very large area, thus making communication and the distribution of supplies difficult. As we had been brought to this delightful part of France for field firing practices, there was not much time for rest or recreation, but the ranges at Nortleulinghem (some five kilometres from Moulle) were excellent, and the training interesting enough.

The other feature of our stay at Moulle—and at Zuytpeene, where we marched *via* St. Omer, Arques and Bavinchove on February 17th—was a series of competitions. C Company (Captain Francis Wortley) had done remarkably well in all recent competitions, both military and sporting, and now proceeded to win fresh laurels. On February 14th this company won the Brigade Drill Competition, and on the 21st the Divisional Drill Competition. On the 19th its football team played the 245th M.G. Company in the semi-final of the Divisional Inter-Company Football Competition, and won 4-0. On the 15th the Battalion team played the 1/3rd (W.R.) Field Ambulance in the final of the Brigade Football Competition, but after a stiff tussle the Ambulance defeated us 1-0.

On the 18th, at Zuytpeene, the Hallamshires held a cross-country run, but it was discovered that a twenty-six kilometre march on the day before is scarcely the best preparation for such an event. On the 20th 2nd Lieutenant S. E. Warburton and A Company Rifle

(1) As a consequence of this re-organization, the 1/5th K.O.Y.L.I. were, to our great regret, transferred from the 148th Brigade to the 62nd Division.

1918. FEBRUARY—MARCH.
Grenade Team won the Divisional Rifle Bombing Competition, while Lieutenant Ryan, with the Scouts, won the Divisional Observing Competition and gained second place in Scouting.

While the Battalion was at Moulle, Major Holmes left for the Senior Officers' School at Aldershot, where he was retained as an instructor.

(f) More of the Salient.

The Battalion entrained at Bavinchove on February 23rd, and was taken up to Ypres, where it was billeted in the ruins of the famous Infantry Barracks. There we stayed for a week doing work under the Engineers and also improving our billets. There was an excellent Divisional Officers' Club on the Menin Road, where one could enjoy the comfort of a real coal fire, a "gin and it," or a shampoo; and there was a very good canteen for the men where they could buy beer, boot-laces, buttons, and many other things, according to their fancy—or thirst.

On March 2nd we marched up to the front line in the Judge Cross Roads sector, east of Polygon Wood, relieving the 6th West Ridings. The trenches had been dug by some New Zealand battalions, and bore traces of this in their names—Papanui, Otaki, Patu, etc. For the first day or two in the line the enemy was comparatively quiet, but on March 5th he opened a very heavy bombardment upon the 37th Division on our right. The bombardment extended over the whole of that division's front from the trenches to the back area, and the shelling on our own front had shown a decided increase. It was well known that the enemy had been preparing a big attack, and when the bombardment continued on the 6th and 7th we naturally thought that the Boche had selected us as his victims.

At 5-15 p.m. on March 7th Captain Unsworth reported that the enemy was showing great activity on the Becelaere—Zwaanhoek Ridge. We had a very good forward observation post in a crater on A Company's front, and from this place a large number of the enemy could be seen, apparently massing for the attack. The artillery were at once 'phoned, and a destructive fire was promptly put on to the enemy troops, with the result that the attack did not materialise. By 7 p.m. all was quiet. Next day the enemy artillery fire was intense all the afternoon, and at 5-45 p.m. he attacked the 37th Division on our immediate right under cover of a smoke barrage. The Germans obtained a temporary footing in the front line, but were ejected by the 10th Royal Fusiliers after a stiff fight. The attack did not extend to

1918. MARCH.

our front, but our artillery co-operated. We expected our turn to come at any moment, and the rather melodramatic messages that we received from the Staff did nothing to increase the general confidence in our ability to repel the attack. No man ever had his feet warmed by being reminded that England expected him not to get them cold.

On the night of March 10th we were relieved in the front line by the 6th West Ridings, and we filed out down the duck-board tracks to the area of Westhoek Ridge. In the somewhat lively eight days from March 2nd to 9th we had only eight men wounded. Battalion Headquarters and two companies were now billeted in tunnelled dug-outs on the Ridge; and the remaining two companies in Railway Wood dug-outs. These were all shell-proof, but there was considerable danger from gas-shelling. Westhoek Ridge was literally covered with guns, and the enemy shelling at this point was often quite disconcerting. Nevertheless, we managed to put in a little time at physical drill, etc., until aeroplane photographs showed that the Ridge was beginning to look like a barrack square. We were then ordered to "scarify" the surface of the ground in order that the guileless Boche might think that no one lived there.

We managed to get the men bathed during our "rest" in these vile dug-outs, but very little real work was done there. The men wrote thousands of letters, and kept the officers busy censoring them—otherwise there was very little to do but sleep. Even that was not easy, for although the vitiated atmosphere of the dug-outs induced sleep, the crashing efforts of our guns prevented it. On March 18th the 4th West Ridings relieved us in the dug-outs, and we moved forward to our old sector in the front line.

We were instructed that the enemy was to be annoyed as much as possible, and that efforts were to be made to secure identifications. A raid was promptly arranged, and Lieutenant Warburton was selected to lead it. The raiding party, according to our usual custom, was sent down to train and rest behind the front line area, and the Scouts made several reconnaissances of the position to be raided. The enemy shelling was heavy every day, particularly on our right front and support lines, and in our first four days we lost twelve men killed and twenty-four wounded. March 21st, the day on which the Boche attacked the Fifth Army in the South, was particularly lively, and at about 9 p.m. the shelling had developed into a veritable barrage. Our Scouts were caught in a heavy gas shoot on their way up to the line, but carried out their patrol "according to plan," and were fired on by the very machine guns which were to be the objective of our raiders.

On March 25th, our last night in the line, our raid took place. The Scout Officer laid tapes from the front line up to within a few yards of the enemy post, and led the various detachments of the raiders into their positions. Colonel Branson, who had returned from leave in time to supervise the arrangements for the raid, came up to the crater in the front line to watch the show, and punctually to the second the artillery opened out with whizz-bangs on the enemy machine gun post. The night was almost perilously moonlit, but the enemy was taken completely by surprise, and in a very few minutes our men returned with four live Boche and two machine guns. They had also killed several Huns and damaged his machine - gun position considerably. Our total casualties for the raid were 2nd Lieutenant Warburton and seven men wounded. Not until the Battalion was out of the line on the next day did we learn that Lieutenant Warburton's servant, who had been watching the raid from the crater, was missing. It transpired that he had attempted to follow Warburton, and had doubtless got lost and killed.

For gallantry in connection with the raid, the M.C. was awarded to 2nd Lieutenant S. E. Warburton, M.M.; the D.C.M. to Sergeant C. Firth; and the M.M. to Corporal F. Lupton and Privates Barron, Day, Adey, Peart and Hopkinson.

We were relieved in the afternoon of the 26th by the 6th West Ridings and marched back to Maui Camp, west of Ypres. Here we spent one night and then returned to the front, relieving the 37th Division south of the Menin Road, almost the only sector in the salient which the Division had not previously visited. The enemy break-through on the Fifth Army Front had made it necessary to withdraw divisions from the northern portion of our line and hurriedly despatch them southwards. Even the vital Ypres Salient was so weakened in men and guns that, had the enemy attacked there, the consequences might have been very serious.

On reaching the line we took over the whole of the front of the 4th Middlesex and part of that of the 8th Somerset L.I., holding our front line with two companies only. The posts were very far apart, and the troops on our right were a scratch battalion of cyclists, cavalry, etc., who were very elated to be in the front line, but had little or no knowledge of infantry warfare. There were plenty of Boche to be seen in the enemy lines, and our snipers had some excellent shooting. We reported to our artillery that the enemy troops were in the habit of wearing soft caps instead of their tin hats, and were gratified to find that several heavy bursts of shrapnel over their heads had a good effect upon such bad trench discipline.

Fortunately for us, the enemy was very quiet on our part of the front. He caused us a certain amount of trouble at first by firing light trench mortars very accurately at our lines, but this was stopped by sending back six of our Stokes to each of his L.T.M.'s. The front was vigorously patrolled throughout each night, but very little was heard except the lurid language of our men as they worked on the barbed wire defences.

Late on the night of April 1st we were relieved by the 7th West Yorkshire Regiment, and went down those interminable duck-board tracks to a point where a miniature train was waiting to take us out to Dickebusch (Scottish Wood Camp).

The news of the Boche attacks in the South led us to suppose that it would not be long before we were taking our share in the task of stopping him, and after the Battalion had had one more (rather uneventful) spell in the line, the Division was withdrawn.

CHAPTER XII

NEUVE EGLISE

(See Map 1)

THIS book is not concerned with the problem of how far the Versailles Council misjudged the direction of the German offensive of 1918; how far the unity of command would have altered the situation had it been established earlier; whether the Fifth Army was unprepared; or why the British Cabinet failed to supply reinforcements when they were demanded.

It did concern the 49th Division, however, that on March 21st Ludendorff attacked the Fifth and Third Armies south of Arras, and in a few days undid the work of months. This meant taking over a larger front in Flanders so that reinforcements might be sent south, and, sooner or later, the Division might expect to form part of those reinforcements. But "the most formidable offensive in the history of the world" (1) began to abate, and on April 9th was launched the second offensive, which began between Armentières and the La Bassée Canal and quickly spread towards Ypres.

In his despatch dated 20th July, 1918, Sir Douglas Haig said:

"The possibility of a German attack north of the La Bassée Canal, for which certain preparations appeared to have been carried out, had been brought to my notice prior to the 21st March. Indications that preparations for a hostile attack in this sector were nearing completion had been observed in the first days of April, but its extent and force could not be accurately gauged.

"There were obvious advantages for the enemy in such a course of action. . . . . .

"It must be remembered that before the northern battle commenced forty-six out of my total force of fifty-eight divisions had been engaged in the southern area. . . . .

"The steps which I could take, however, to meet a danger which I could foresee were limited by the fact that, though the enemy's progress on the Somme had for the time being been stayed, the great

(1) Professor Pollard: " Short History of the Great War."

mass of hostile divisions still concentrated on that front constituted a threat to the safety of the British Armies of an imperative character. The enemy was in a position to take immediate advantage of any weakening of my forces in that area."

After penetrating the British line from Armentières to La Bassée to a depth of some four miles on the 9th, the Germans captured Estaires and carried the attack northwards towards Messines on the 10th. On the same day British troops were compelled to withdraw from Armentières. Merville fell on the 11th, and "meanwhile, north of Armentières strong hostile attacks had developed towards midday, and were pressed vigorously in the direction of Nieppe and Neuve Eglise. In the afternoon fierce fighting took place about Messines.

"Owing to the progress made by the enemy in the Ploegsteert sector, the position of the 34th Division at Nieppe, where they had beaten off a determined attack during the morning, became untenable. Accordingly in the early part of the night our troops at Nieppe fell back under orders to the neighbourhood of Pont d'Achelles. Still further to shorten our line and economise men, our troops between Pont d'Achelles and Wytschaete were withdrawn to positions about 1,000 yards east of Neuve Eglise and Wulverghem. This withdrawal involved the abandonment of Hill 63 and of the positions still held by us about Messines."

* * * * * *

On the morning of April 9th the Brigadier called together all his officers and gave them a few hints on the probable movements of the Brigade in the near future. It appeared that we were to go down to the Somme area. Some of the remnants of divisions who had been "through it" were now up in Flanders, and we heard many tales of the fighting. Most of us had been soundly trained for open warfare in the early days of the war, and that training had been constantly refreshed during periods of rest from the line, but years of trench warfare had made some of us think that open fighting was all very well in theory, but of little practical value for this war. Now we saw officers whose kits had been captured by the Boche, and heard stories of subalterns commanding battalions, of transport men defending their limbers with their own rifle fire, of advanced and rear-guard actions, and of lines of men advancing and retiring in the prescribed Field Service Regulations manner.

On this very day the Boche made the attack on the Neuve Chapelle sector held by the Portuguese. The heavy firing could be

1918. APRIL.

heard throughout the day, and towards evening there came the first news of the Portuguese rout. The Battalion travelled that same evening by train to Albert Camp, near Reninghelst. Our programme of proceeding to the Somme area still held good, and everybody was in high spirits.

At 6 a.m. on April 10th information was received that our move to the Somme was cancelled, and that we were to be flung into the breach caused by the Portuguese Army's collapse. We at once packed up and shortly after 9 a.m. were in lorries on the road to Neuve Eglise.

After leaving Dranoutre our progress was very slow, as the road was packed with traffic of all kinds proceeding in the opposite direction. There were many civilian refugees from the area which had been overrun by the Boche, and they presented a very pathetic picture as they trudged along. Old men, women and children drove farm carts or pushed a wheelbarrow piled high with odds and ends from their homes. Others had been unable to carry away anything save the feather mattress so dear to the heart of the Flemish peasant. Several heavy guns, drawn by caterpillar tractors, passed slowly down the road. The sight of these going back did not tend to make us very cheerful, for big guns, just as certainly as straws, show which way the wind is blowing.

We reached the vicinity of Neuve Eglise at about 1 p.m. and bivouacked in a field two or three hundred yards north-west of the village, the situation being such that we did not know whether we should be left in the field for half-an-hour or half a week. Some apparently deserted tents a few hundred yards away were appropriated and the whole Battalion put comfortably under canvas. Battalion Headquarters had a wooden hut, where the constant arrival and departure of runners showed that the occupants were having a busy time. A number of officers and men, who were to be left out of the battle to act as reinforcements when necessary, were now sent away.

Precautions against surprise were taken by keeping strong parties of men constantly patrolling the roads and ground east of the village. The enemy was working his way along the valley of the river Douve, and by mid-day on the 10th he had captured Ploegsteert Village and part of the Wood. He had also taken Messines, but that was recaptured later in the day by the South African Brigade. When night came the artillery fire increased. Few enemy lights were to be seen, but a great blaze a couple of miles to the south marked the burn-

1918. APRIL.

ing village of Steenwerck. There were still a few civilians in Neuve Eglise, and one estaminet was actually open and doing a roaring trade in beer. These civilians were cleared out during the night by the military police.(1)

At 4 a.m. on April 11th the C.O. sent a large patrol, consisting of two officers and some forty men, to reconnoitre the ground east of the village. This party found it possible to proceed some 2,000 yards to the hamlet of L'Alouette, but were held up there by a heavy enemy barrage. There was no sign of any British troops in the vicinity, and the enemy shelling did no damage, although it proved to us that the Boche did not know what line was held by the British. The patrol returned to Neuve Eglise at 6 a.m., bringing four Germans who had been found in the charge of one very sleepy Tommy. This man had removed his boots, puttees, and socks, and was warming his feet before a wood fire in a ruined house, with the four Huns sitting or lying on the floor about him; his rifle and bayonet were in a corner of the room, and the Germans were perfectly at liberty to kill their guard and walk back to their lines had they been so inclined!

During the morning of April 12th the Battalion was warned to be ready to move at a moment's notice. At 11-45 a.m. the Colonel was hurriedly summoned to Brigade Headquarters, where he was told that the enemy had broken through in squares T22 and T23. This was an area one thousand by two thousand yards, situate about half-way between "Plugstreet" Wood and Neuve Eglise. The C.O. received verbal operation orders, which might be reduced to six words—"Move forward and restore the situation." A few moments later the Battalion marched out of the village by platoons at intervals, protected by a screen of scouts, advanced guard and flank guards, as practised so often, but never before in "the real thing." On arrival at L'Alouette we found a very peaceful-looking countryside, with no sign of either friend or foe. The ground fell away to the east in a succession of gently undulating meadows and ploughed fields, divided by ditches, which were in many cases both wide and deep. Four machine guns from our Divisional M.G. Corps were allotted to us to assist in the attack.

On leaving Neuve Eglise the C.O. had been told that the Battalion would be under the orders of the 25th Division, but nothing

(1) It is interesting to note that on this day (April 10th) we had only one officer (Colonel Branson) and eighty other ranks who landed in France on April 13th, 1915, and who had served with the Battalion continuously since.

was known of the location of any of their Brigade Headquarters. A Brigade Headquarters (but not of the 25th Division) was found by chance near L'Alouette, but the Colonel who was in charge knew nothing of the situation to his front, though he stated that he had a battalion on Hill 63, a commanding position on our left. He was told what our orders were, and gave us his blessing, but took no further interest in us until a couple of hours later, when we received a message that as the battalion on Hill 63 had now been put under someone else's command, his Headquarters "would cease to function forthwith," and that left us entirely on our own once more. Later in the evening we were glad to hear that we were again under our own Brigadier.

After a few minutes spent in plotting out the line of our advance, the Battalion moved forward. B Company (Payne) and C (L. W. Johnson) had been detailed as the front line of the attack, A (Unsworth) and D (Mainprice) being held back near Battalion Headquarters. They moved across the open country in artillery formation. It was now about 3 p.m., and the sun was shining brightly. The men advanced as steadily and kept their formation as well as if they were on a "field day" practice in England. During the advance the enemy shelling was weak and ineffective, and caused no casualties, but after proceeding about a thousand yards the two companies came under the fire of rifles and machine guns from a line of farms along a road about four hundred yards away. Our men at once deployed into line and advanced by platoon and section rushes until they reached the road. After a short, sharp fight the enemy was driven back from his farmhouse posts and our men consolidated along the line of the road. This position had been won at a cost of one man killed, eight wounded and two missing. 2nd Lieutenants Parker and Nicholls were also wounded, and the latter officer died of his wounds shortly afterwards. We obtained touch on the left with the K.S.L.I. (19th Division) and the 25th Division M.G.C., but our right flank was in the air. D Company was, therefore, hurriedly pushed up to form a flank.

About 6 p.m. B Company signalled that they could see cavalry advancing on their front, but these did not materialise. Shortly afterwards the enemy drove the troops on our left from Hill 63 and opened a heavy bombardment on our front. This shelling was not followed by an attack, but at 7-15 p.m. the Battalion was ordered to withdraw about two thousand yards to the north and take up the line of the road near Keepaway Farm. This was a very sound order, for we had never found touch on our right, and we had just seen the Hun occupy a

1918. April.

commanding position on our left, but it was a task of no little difficulty, as the night was exceptionally dark—companies had to move by compass across entirely unknown ground intersected by many deep ditches, and the enemy were in close touch. It was not until 11 p.m. that all our men were in position, with the 4th K.O.Y.L.I. on our right and the 4th K.S.L.I. on our left. Everybody worked hard to get "dug-in" before daylight, by which time a useful line of trenches had been constructed.

At about midnight Colonel Branson met the C.O. of the 4th K.S.L.I., who stated that he had orders to retire to the Army Reserve Line behind; this he did, leaving our left flank this time in the air. Later on our flank was protected, to a certain extent, by the men of the 458th Company R.E., with the addition of stragglers of infantry from several different regiments. Our left company was attacked twice during the night by patrols, but the enemy was beaten off.

Soon after dawn on April 12th an enemy 'plane came over our lines, flying very low. The machine was received by a veritable hail of bullets from our rifles and Lewis guns, and in a very short time it crashed within a few yards of our line. The pilot was found to be quite dead and the observer badly wounded. He was lifted out of the wrecked machine and carried down to our aid post near Battalion Headquarters. The stretcher party was fired on by Boche machine - gunners, but managed to get the wounded airman to the aid post, where he died shortly afterwards.

During the day we saw numbers of the enemy in small parties, and enjoyed some very good shooting. The Hythe experts would have been delighted to see the "Indication and Recognition of Targets" training being put to such excellent use.

At 3 p.m. we at last obtained touch on our left with the 9th R.I.F. (36th Division). The enemy opened a heavy bombardment at 6 p.m. in the neighbourhood of Wulverghem, and the troops on our left could be seen retiring. This state of affairs continued until 8 p.m., when the bombardment spread to the 4th K.O.Y.L.I. on our right. In a few more minutes the enemy had broken through the left company of the K.O.Y.L.I., and we were being attacked from our right flank. At the same time a heavy attack was launched against our left front (C Company). The enemy were in vastly superior numbers, and as both our flanks were turned, we were compelled to withdraw—slowly, but fighting all the way. The battle was fought entirely by bullet, bomb and bayonet, and the crash of many thousands of rifles made an

1918. APRIL.

appalling noise. In spite of the fact that many men were shooting too high, the execution amongst the Boche must have been very great.

The machine-gunners who were attached to us did splendid work. One gunner remained firing into the packed ranks of the enemy until they swarmed past him, then got back, and was in our new line in a few minutes pouring out another hail of bullets.

By midnight we had the enemy held up, and although the Battalion had been fighting very large odds for four hours, outflanked on both sides, we had withdrawn no more than five hundred yards. In this fighting Lieutenant Bedwell and 2nd Lieutenants Howells and J. F. Dixon were killed.

Our position was then some three hundred yards east of the Neuve Eglise—Wulverghem Road. A company of the 4th K.O.Y.L.I. was placed at the disposal of the Battalion, and was used to prolong our right sufficiently to get into touch with the Army Reserve Line of trenches to the south-west of our position, where were the remainder of the K.O.Y.L.I.

At 2 a.m. next morning orders were received to withdraw to the Army Reserve Line. This move was completed by 4 a.m., A and D Companies being in the line, with B and C Companies dug in a short distance behind. The 8th Gloucesters were in the line on our left, and the 4th K.S.L.I. and 4th K.O.Y.L.I. on our right. The enemy by this time had broken through again beyond the K.O.Y.L.I. on our right, and parties of Boche were seen in the west end of Neuve Eglise, thus taking us in the rear. A party of fifty men, under Captain Wortley and Lieutenant Gifford, was sent to attempt to drive the enemy out. This task was very successfully accomplished. The Boche was driven from the village, leaving behind many dead and no fewer than fifty-one prisoners, including a battalion commander. Captain Wortley then established his party on a line south of the village and strengthened it with fragments of battalions of the 100th Brigade, who were in the vicinity. During the day the troops on our right were driven back a short distance, and the enemy again obtained a hold on the western outskirts of the village.

At 7 p.m. we were ordered to dig in facing south-east near the Wulverghem Road, in order to connect up with the K.O.Y.L.I., who had by this time been compelled to retire from the Army Line owing to their right flank being in the air. Our positions in the Army Line were taken over by the K.S.L.I., and by 8-30 p.m. we had formed a line on the new position. Half-an-hour earlier Captain J. F. Wortley had been killed whilst leading a party of about forty stragglers of another division back into the line. He had fought and worked magnificently throughout the battle, and seemed to bear a charmed life. As a Company Commander for many months, and as a Second-in-Command in what was certainly the most critical time of the war, he had been of immense service to the Battalion. He was one of those exceptional officers, equally good at training his men behind the line and at commanding them in action.

When darkness came again the enemy flares seemed to be creeping nearer and nearer. Our position was getting very precarious. We were in grave danger of being outflanked, and the situation in the west end of the village was most obscure. The enemy were firing machine guns at us from some of the houses, though odd parties of another British division were certainly holding isolated points. To meet the situation, 2nd Lieutenant Hope and twenty men were taken to a point about forty yards from the village and dug in as an outpost. Behind this party we had a line consisting of the Headquarters Details of our Battalion and of the 4th K.O.Y.L.I., facing south-west. On the left the K.S.L.I. were still in the Army Line facing, roughly, east, while the Hallamshires—facing nearly south—filled the gap between the K.S.L.I. and the K.O.Y.L.I. at the east end of the village.

When the dawn came it was seen that the enemy had penetrated well into the village. The C.O. went to see the battalion on our right (100th Brigade) with a view to organising a counter-attack, but their headquarters could not be found. A Company was moved round to form a defensive flank to the right, as we were now all but surrounded by the enemy. Officers and men were very battle-weary with the incessant strain of the past four days. We needed reinforcements—and needed them badly—but none came. Our losses already amounted to two hundred and fifty men and twelve officers, while the party left out of the battle, in reserve, had already been used up by the Brigade in another sector. The situation was extremely critical, and the position was rapidly becoming untenable. In the absence, however, of orders to retire, the C.O. had no alternative but to attempt to hold on.

About noon it was reported that there was still a British Battalion Headquarters in the west end of the village. This seemed incredible, as the village was almost completely in the hands of the enemy, but the Scout Officer was told to investigate the matter. Accordingly, he proceeded to the village, and, after a few mild excite-

1918. APRIL.

ments, reached the School House. To his amazement, he found a complete Battalion Headquarters Staff in the large cellar of the house. He explained the situation to them, accepted with gratitude a cup of cocoa from the Adjutant, and departed with great haste.

The tenacity of these people was rewarded by special mention in the official report as having maintained themselves in Neuve Eglise until 2 p.m. on April 14th. As a matter of fact, it was several hours after this when the Hallamshires and K.O.Y.L.I. were compelled to leave the east end of the village.

At 6 p.m. the enemy again attacked after a heavy bombardment with artillery and trench mortars. The attack was launched against the Hallamshires, K.O.Y.L.I. and K.S.L.I., and extended a long way to our right; again the line was put in jeopardy by the brigade on the right flank giving way. When the enemy were seen to be in possession of a mill, which was a few hundred yards to our right rear, it was clear that Neuve Eglise could no longer be held, and the Battalion and the K.O.Y.L.I., under a very heavy machine-gun fire from the village, withdrew about 400 yards, where, still under a heavy machine-gun fire, we dug in. The country was very open, and there was hardly any cover from fire or view, but the men used their entrenching tools with tremendous energy, and soon had the few inches of cover which made all the difference. Meanwhile, those who were not digging had been busily pumping lead into any Boche who showed themselves, but most of the enemy remained behind the cover of the houses.

At about 6-30 p.m. the Colonel was wounded by a bullet in the arm. We maintained our position until 4-30 a.m., when the Brigade Major (Captain Moxsy) came in person to order us to withdraw to the main railway line some twelve hundred yards north of Neuve Eglise, where Captain G. Unsworth took command of the Battalion.

At 6 a.m. we were withdrawn from this line to the south-west of Mont Kemmel, where we bivouacked—and called the roll. We had had five days of incessant strain and hard fighting, and the bill was a heavy one. The Battalion had lost 131 killed and missing, and 173 wounded, including Captain J. F. Wortley, M.C., Lieutenants C. T. Bedwell, T. E. Sanderson and S. H. Reynolds, 2nd Lieutenants A. J. Nicholls, J. F. Dixon and D. Howells, killed; Lieutenant-Colonel D. S. Branson, D.S.O., M.C., Major J. D. Kerr, M.C., Captain L. Cheesewright, Lieutenants R. E. Mainprice and W. Ryan, 2nd

1918. April.

Lieutenants E. Williams, C. G. Millar, S. R. Hirst, P. H. Stockley, M.M., W. K. Shopland and J. B. Parker, wounded.

Lieutenant C. Utley was captured by the enemy, and Lieutenant W. N. Scawin and 2nd Lieutenant H. R. Key were missing, and are now presumed to have been killed.

* * * * * *

We were not allowed to remain "resting" near Kemmel Hill for many hours. At 12-35 a.m. the following morning we were ordered to proceed at once to an assembly position about three kilometres away. On arrival there we were halted at a farmhouse, and the men were billeted in a large stable, with Battalion Headquarters in the house. Here it was we met the 5th Y. and L. again. This battalion had been attached to the 74th Brigade (25th Division) from the 10th April, and had done extraordinarily good work in the fighting near Steenwerck, some miles away from us. The G.O.C. 74th Brigade "was much impressed by the dashing manner in which the Battalion carried out the attack on Cabaret du Saule on the 11th April, and by its stubborn resistance on the 14th April on Mont de Lille." Our chief regret at this time was that the 49th Division was not allowed to fight as a unit. The 147th Brigade had been moved to help the 34th Division in the neighbourhood of Armentières; the 146th Brigade fought on Kemmel Hill, sending one battalion (the 7th W. Yorks.) to assist the 62nd Infantry Brigade in the Messines sector; while the 5th Y. and L.'s were detached from the 148th Brigade, as has been shown. At the same time, the 49th Divisional Artillery were being employed in the retreat in the Salient.

At 6 a.m. we received orders to take up a position along a line of posts running east and west across the Locre—Bailleul Road. We had the 8th Leicesters on our left and the 4th K.O.Y.L.I. on our right. The situation in front of our line was still doubtful.

In the evening of the 17th the Battalion relieved parts of the 9th H.L.I. and 16th K.R.R. in the line about a thousand to fifteen hundred yards south-west of Dranoutre. The troops on our left were a heterogeneous collection of infantry, cavalry, cyclists, corps troops and men from schools and reinforcement camps, under the command of Brigadier-General L. J. Wyatt, our one-time Commanding Officer. This scratch body of troops made a great name for themselves during the April fighting as "Wyatt's Mixed Force."

At 8 o'clock on the morning of April 18th the enemy shelled Battalion Headquarters and set the farmhouse on fire, causing a

1918. APRIL.

migration to another cellar in the vicinity, but he was comparatively quiet throughout the next two days. Late at night on the 19th we were relieved by the 83rd French Infantry Regiment—one of several French battalions sent up at this time to help in relieving the pressure on the British front. Considering the difficulties of language, the relief was carried out very expeditiously by 2 a.m. We marched some nine kilometres to a field about two thousand yards west of Reninghelst, and bivouacked. We were so utterly weary that even food was neglected, and we slept for several hours. Later in the day the Battalion marched to Ridge Camp, near Brandhoek, and found very good billets in huts. During the last four days in the line we had lost six men killed and thirty-four wounded. 2nd Lieutenant F. W. Davidson, M.M., and Lieutenant D. T. Keating were both killed on April 17th.

M. Clemenceau inspected a party of two hundred of our men on April 21st on the Poperinghe—Vlamertinghe road, near the camp. Captain R. E. Wilson was recalled from the Army School on April 22nd, and he now took command of the Battalion with the rank of Lieutenant-Colonel, while Captain Unsworth was appointed Second-in-Command. We also received a draft of six officers.

Until April 24th our time was spent in re-fitting and re-organising companies. A certain amount of training was carried out, particularly in practice of the leap-frog method of attack. We thought it possible that we should be given a rest from the line, at least until we had received a good draft of men, as our strength was only about five hundred all told. However, at 3-15 a.m. on April 25th an order warned us to be ready to move at thirty minutes' notice, and at 1 p.m. the Battalion marched forward to an assembly position near Ouderdom. We stayed in a field for nearly twelve hours, and at 12-30 a.m. on the 26th moved up to the front line. Our orders were to take over the "Blue" line for a distance of about four hundred yards south of the Vierstraat—Hallebast Road, from which position we were to make an attack shortly after arrival.

By the time we had reached our appointed position it was 3-30 a.m. The 5th Y. and L. were on our right and the XXII. Corps Mounted Troops on the left. Our information was to the effect that a counter-attack would be carried out by the 39th French Division on the right and by the 25th British Division on the left. Our Brigade was ordered to push forward at the same time for a distance of about eight hundred yards behind a barrage and to take the La Polka—Vierstraat Line.

1918. April.

At 4-25 a.m. the attack took place. Orders stated that we should meet with no opposition short of our objective, and the artillery programme was based on this assumption. The "barrage" proved to be ludicrously inadequate, and was indeed almost unnoticed. Fortunately, there was a heavy mist, which covered the beginning of our advance, but very soon we encountered a line of machine guns (well on our side of the barrage) which poured out such an annihilating fire that it was impossible to continue the attack, and we were forced to withdraw to our original line. In this short operation we lost seven officers and ninety-one men. Captain H. Faulder, Lieutenant T. P. Bradbury, 2nd Lieutenants P. P. McArdle and R. J. R. Penrose were killed; 2nd Lieutenant W. Beck, D.C.M., was missing, now presumed killed; and Lieutenants Gifford and Payne were wounded. Our casualties in the ranks were seventeen killed, nine missing and sixty-five wounded.

The Boche might be expected to attack at any time, and his activity during the next two or three days was not calculated to add to our sense of security. For two hours later in the same morning, and for an hour in the afternoon, the whole Brigade area was shelled. At dusk the Battalion took over a further one hundred and fifty yards of front from the 5th Y. and L. in order to enable them to fill a gap in their right flank. Next morning at 4-45 a.m. the enemy artillery fire increased to the violent state, which the Boche called "drum-fire," but, apparently, it was only a counter-preparation shoot. This bombardment was repeated at dusk, but still no enemy action followed. Later in the evening we were relieved by the 2nd Royal Scots, and took up positions in support; one company was in close support to the 5th Y. and L., and the remainder were about five hundred yards from the front line, with Battalion Headquarters in a building officially known as "Bloody Farm." On April 28th the enemy repeated his bombardment for an hour at dusk, and a message was sent by the 4th K.O.Y.L.I. (who had taken over the front on the right of the 5th Y. and L.) to the effect that the enemy was preparing to attack. Shortly afterwards a further message came through that this was not the case on our part of the front.

At 5-30 next morning, after a very heavy bombardment, the enemy attacked on the front held by 4th K.O.Y.L.I. and 5th Y. and L. The Germans came over in massed formation with fixed bayonets, and were met by a furious fire from rifles and Lewis guns. The enemy pressed forward with great determination, and, in spite of fearful losses in his packed ranks, he succeeded, by sheer force of numbers, in effecting a lodgment at the junction of the two regiments. The O.C. 5th Y. and L. called upon the Hallamshires to counter-attack and eject the enemy. We prepared at once to do this, but in the meantime the Boche had been driven out by the troops holding the line. The Lewis gun teams of our close support company were able to give valuable assistance in repelling the attack and restoring the situation. The enemy kept up an intermittent bombardment throughout the day, and was frequently reported to be massing, but no further attack developed. Enemy aeroplanes had been extremely active all day, but were not flying low enough to give the infantrymen any sport. April 30th, our last day in the line, was quiet, and at night we were relieved by the 9th Loyal North Lancs. The relief was complete by 1-30 a.m., and we marched out to a camp near Reninghelst, having lost during the five days seven officers and one hundred and fourteen other ranks.

At the end of the month we were reinforced by a draft of ten officers, three of whom were lent to us by the 19th Lancashire Fusiliers, the Divisional Pioneer Battalion.

We stayed at the camp for one day only, marching back to the line on May 2nd, and taking over the front on the right of our previous position from the 3rd Worcesters. Before the relief was actually completed a party of about six of the enemy were seen approaching our line. Largely owing to the gallantry of Private E. Hopkinson (of A Company), the party was dispersed, two of the enemy being killed and one captured. Two bags of mail and some rations were also captured, the former proving as valuable to the Intelligence Department as the latter did to Private Hopkinson and his comrades. Hopkinson already wore the M.M. for his work on a raid a few weeks before; he was now awarded a bar to the medal.

Information given by Boche prisoners—including the man captured by us on the previous night—pointed to a probable attack on May 3rd. Sure enough, at about 8-15 p.m., a very heavy bombardment opened out away to our right. Shortly afterwards this spread to our front, and continued until 9 p.m. No attack was made on our front, however, though the enemy made a strong effort to regain the village of Locre on our right.

Next day we were again informed that Boche prisoners had given warning of a further attack, but nothing developed. We were relieved in the evening by the 143rd French Infantry Regiment, and trekked wearily out to a camp near Busseboom. Except for the impression that we were about to make our very last stand—conveyed to us by telegrams and sudden accesses of artillery fury, we had "enjoyed" a comparatively quiet time in the line and had lost only four men killed and ten wounded. Lieutenant C. N. Platt and 2nd Lieutenant F. H. Oldfield were both wounded, after being with the Battalion for four days only.

On the morning of May 5th we marched to a camp near St. Jan ter Biezen, about four kilometres west of Poperinghe. Here nine officers of the Loyal North Lancashire Regiment joined the Battalion, so that we now had a fairly strong muster of officers, but only four hundred and seventy-three men, including transport and all details. We were deficient in Lewis guns and nearly every other item of equipment. The men's clothing was more or less in rags, and everybody needed a bath very badly. For the next few days, therefore, little was done beyond making up these deficiencies, re-fitting and equipping the men, and getting them re-clothed and bathed. A certain amount of training was carried out under company arrangements, particularly in the Lewis gun, as we had lost so many men of the teams that it was vitally important to train others to replace them. With the exception of Lieutenant-Colonel R. E. Wilson, Major Unsworth, Captain P. A. Branson, Captain D. P. Grant, Captain W. Ryan and Lieutenant Driver, all our officers were new to the Battalion and most of them had never been under fire. On May 9th we were joined by five officers and thirteen men from our Second Line Battalion, and three days later we received a very useful draft of one hundred and twenty men from England. They were not well-trained by any means, but fortunately we still had several good N.C.O. instructors left, and training went on very satisfactorily.

The Boche bombing 'planes came over every evening as soon as it was dark. Many bombs were dropped in the vicinity, but none closely enough to worry us. This quiet life of work and play continued until the 19th, when, after the customary delay of several hours, the Battalion was packed into lorries and taken to a big field about ten kilometres from St. Omer. Here we pitched tents and thanked Providence for a breath of fresh air and a glimpse of the countryside where there were no shell-holes or trenches. We had been brought to this place for musketry practice, and that always meant work from dawn to dusk. Fortunately for us, the ranges were quite close to our camp, and we were able to utilise all our time in shooting instead of wasting half of each day by marching to and from the

1918. May.

range. We had four days' shooting, including one day's field firing near Moulle.

Further drafts of men, totalling nearly two hundred, joined us now, and on parade we once more looked like a battalion and not a company. The Adjutant, Captain D. P. Grant, went into hospital, sick, on May 23rd, and was transferred to England. His successor was Captain P. A. Branson, the Transport Officer.

We returned to Road Camp at St. Jan ter Biezen by train, detraining at Proven. Next day we marched back to Proven and were billeted in huts which had previously been occupied by Chinese labourers. The camps were called "Peterboro" and "Pekin," but they were known only as "Chink Camp."

The authorities signified their approval of the fight put up by the Battalion in April by the award of a number of decorations. Colonel Branson was awarded a bar to his D.S.O., Lieutenant W. D. G. Gifford received a bar to his M.C., Captains D. P. Grant and L. W. Johnson, 2nd Lieutenants H. Payne and C. R. Hope were awarded the M.C. The D.C.M. was given to C.S.M. W. Cadman, A/C.S.M. G. Pearson and Sergeant J. Davison; the M.M. to Sergeant F. Baker; Corporals S. Fell and G. Hudson; Lance-Corporals C. Ogden, C. Lawrence, T. York, A. Foster and H. Leaver; Privates H. Jeffery, J. Clark, A. B. Cahill, F. W. Sissons, P. Wray, G. Thickett, J. Andrews, H. Atkinson, A. Bennett, A. Peat, R. Winter, A. H. Neve and F. W. Wharton; and a Bar to the M.M. to Privates E. H. Hopkinson and C. Turtle.

CHAPTER XIII

YPRES ONCE MORE

(See Map 1)

"AT the end of April, 1918, though the onrush of the German Armies had been stemmed for the time being, the situation on the Western Front, and particularly on the British portion of it, was still critical. . . . . .

"In short, the German attacks, though they had failed to break the Allied line, had stretched the resources of the Allies to the uttermost. . . . . .

"In these circumstances, the possibility of an immediate renewal of the enemy's offensive could not but be viewed with grave anxiety. . . . . .

"On the other hand, the enemy had undoubtedly paid heavily for his successes, and had used up a great number of divisions, among them his best and his most highly trained. . . . .

"The period under review (May to November, /18) accordingly divides itself naturally into two main sections. During the first, the policy governing the action of the forces under my command was the maintenance of an active defence, whereby our line might be preserved unbroken, while every opportunity was taken to rest and train our sorely-tried divisions."

Sir D. Haig's Despatch dated 21st December, 1918.

The 49th Division, as one of the "sorely-tried," had to rest, train and "maintain an active defence" in the neighbourhood of Ypres. For us "the possibility of an immediate renewal of the enemy's offensive" was very real. The activity of our defence lay in frequent raids on the enemy trenches, in annoying the Boche whenever possible with gas, and in digging new lines of defence in case they were wanted. Resting was easy enough; training was another problem. At one time during this period 70 per cent. of the Hallamshires had seen no actual fighting, and though anxiety on that score was later proved to be needless, the C.O. was leaving nothing to chance. Lewis-gun teams, for instance, had been made up with inexperienced men, and a Lewis gunner cannot be trained in a day. Finally, in addition to training

1918. MAY.

itself, the Division had to help train some of the American infantry, who had not yet been tried at all.

During the fighting in March and April our line had been withdrawn south of the Ypres Salient so much that it was impossible to retain our positions in the Salient itself. All the ridges which had been won at such fearful cost in the autumn of 1917 were given back to the enemy, and our front line was now only just comfortably clear of Ypres. The glorious wreck of Ypres itself had been out of ordinary shell range when we held Passchendaele, but now it was once more standing just behind our lines. Again the enemy shells pounded the ruins of the fine buildings, and the cellars and dug-outs were filled with poisonous gas. The tower of the Cloth Hall once more became the chief target of Boche gunners, and the Grand Place (or "Wipers Square") a place where one quickened pace.

Of Ypres, as of Verdun, the watchword was "Ils ne passeront pas!", and it is certain that if Prince Rupprecht had launched his much-talked-of attack at Ypres, he would have had the fight of his life. Many of us knew the roads and ruins, the holes and corners of the old town better than our local towns in England. We had slept in the Infantry Barracks and under the Ramparts, had washed in the Canal, bought beer in the Theatre, attended divine service in the Powder Magazine, and had our wounds dressed in the Prison.

Poperinghe was no longer the comfortable place that it was in 1917. Every house and every shop had been evacuated, and the enemy shelled the town consistently. The shopkeepers were allowed back into the town at given times to recover their stock-in-trade, and re-established themselves along the road-sides a mile or two further west in little shacks built of wood, mud, and any corrugated iron or other material which they could beg, borrow or steal from the British Army. Several of these temporary houses were built almost entirely of tin boxes, which had once contained Army biscuits. Here the Belgians sold the atrocious silk post-cards, coarse lace, sandy chocolate and bad beer, for which most of Tommy's money was exchanged.

From Chink Camp we went forward every day to work on a reserve line of trenches which was being constructed east of Poperinghe. This was one of a series of reserve lines which were being built in view of the imminence of Prince Rupprecht's probable attack in the Ypres sector. We moved off at 4 o'clock each morning in a miniature train of trucks on a light railway. Every field was under cultivation, as is usual with the Belgians, who must be serious

1918. MAY.

rivals of the ant in industry. Small coppices were dotted about here and there, and in the distance a gaunt windmill stretched its arms to the sky. Very few farms were to be seen, and one marvelled to see these huge fields producing their various crops, apparently without human aid.

Occasionally the line ran past places where huge craters gaped in the soil—evidence of Hun efforts to hit the narrow snaky track—and sometimes the rush of a big shell would startle one out of the sleepy state which results from rising before the world is aired. After about two pipes—delightful at 4 a.m.—we drew up at a siding, jumped out of the train and thawed ourselves in the time-honoured fashion of the old cabby. Companies then filed off to their various sectors of the trench-line, posted Lewis-gun anti-aircraft guards, and got to work.

By giving the men a specific job, instead of telling them to work for six hours, the amount of work done each day was tremendously increased—and often completed in less than the time allowed. The R.E.'s had learned a lot since the days when they could lead a company of infantry into a crumbling trench three feet deep in mud and water, hand them fifty shovels, and instruct them to "get the water out."

Our work on this reserve line was really quite pleasant, as the soil was very suitable for digging trenches. We were not unduly molested by the Boche, although we were in full view from Kemmel Hill. Scores of "heavies" passed over us to burst with a crash in Poperinghe, where a huge, slowly rising cloud of light-brown dust would indicate that another very desirable dwelling had gone west. When the day's work was finished we lost no time in getting aboard the toy train and starting away, as the "siding" where the train awaited us was often shelled.

During our occupation of Chink Camp several men fell sick with a mysterious illness which we called "Chink Fever." This fever had all the symptoms of the great influenza epidemic which ravaged Europe later in the year, but which at that time was unknown. About fifty men were sent into hospital, but they appeared to have the disease in a mild form, as they all recovered and rejoined the Battalion.

Captain S. Brooke rejoined us at the end of May—and having had only three of the six months' rest in England promised him, he was distinctly annoyed! Another draft of about seventy men, nearly all untrained, reached us at Chink Camp, and in the afternoon of the last day of May we marched forward to M Camp, near Poperinghe,

1918. JUNE.
where the arrival of sixty more men distinctly strained our accommodation.

On June 1st Colonel Wilson and the Company Commanders went up to reconnoitre the new sector which we were about to take over. They found Ypres as quiet as the grave, and as deserted as "No Man's Land." Battalion Headquarters were to be lodged in luxury and safety in the Ramparts near the Menin Gate. These billets had been occupied a few short months before by Divisional Headquarters Staff, and the front line, which passed through Hell Fire Corner and skirted the west bank of Zillebeke Lake, was less than a mile from the town. At 4 p.m. the next afternoon the Battalion paraded for the move up to the line, and marched to a rail-head called "Remy Sidings," where it was packed into the open trucks of a toy train, and was soon clattering and jolting away to the front line area.

During the journey we passed many reminders that Passchendaele was no longer ours. Camps, horse-lines, canteens and baths that had been miles behind the line were now so close that they were entirely deserted—and most of them partially destroyed by the enemy shelling. The train carried us as far as a desolate spot known as "Forward Dump," and from here we marched forward by platoons, with a goodly interval between them. Past the well-named "Suicide Corner" and round by "Salvation Corner," along by the stagnant water of the "Dead End" of the Ypres Canal the platoons disappeared, one by one, into the darkness. We had been ordered to avoid Ypres itself, as it was a veritable shell-trap at night, but two unfortunate companies took the wrong turning in the inky blackness of the night and found themselves marching through Ypres Square. Luckily, they got clear of the town without being caught either by the Boche or the Colonel.

When last we had seen Menin Road it was as thick with traffic as any street in London—now it was silent and deserted, and was crossed at intervals by barriers of sandbags and barbed wire. The Officers' Club at the Menin Gate was merely a broken, blackened hut inhabited only by rats. Our front line was on very familiar ground. Just in front of the parapet on our left company sector could be seen a strange-looking patch of concrete—all that was left of the Cavalry Road Baths, where the men of our Battalion had scraped themselves clean on several occasions during the past winter.

It was nearly midnight before the relief was complete. Day-

1918. JUNE..

light found us distinctly hazy as to the whereabouts of the enemy in case we should want him.

Though a fruitless raid had been carried out the night before the relief, we had been led to understand that it was suicide to attempt to reach the front line in daylight; but we soon came to the conclusion that the Boche held his main line a long distance away, with a few scattered outposts in front.

For the next few days we just endured the dull routine of trench warfare—*i.e.*, the opposing gunners engaged in a pleasant little shooting match—with the infantry of each side as targets. We lost about twenty men as a result of efforts of the Boche in this direction.

The trenches were now in splendid condition, as the dry weather had made all the water and mud disappear. Grass and weeds grew over the parapets, and Nature began to hide the shell-holes in a marvellous way. Even flowers and vegetables appeared here and there, and our company headquarters' dug-outs were usually brightened by a few wild marguerites and poppies stuck into an eighteen-pounder shell case. Near the Ramparts were the remains of what had once been fine gardens, and from them many beautiful roses and other flowers were obtained to grace the tables of Battalion Headquarters.

On June 9th the first party (about two dozen strong) of American Infantry joined us, and were received with very great enthusiasm by our men.

On the night of June 11th we were relieved by the 7th West Yorks. The relief was very late in arriving, and it was not until 5 a.m. that we reached Brake Camp. This was a collection of well-constructed huts built under the cover of a small wood. It had the advantage of being quite close to good parade grounds and baths, but it was also near an important cross-roads and a noisy battery of 9.2's. For the first three days out of the trenches we laboured at burying a cable which ran to Vlamertinghe Chateau, now our Brigade Headquarters. In spite of the fact that it was less than four miles from the enemy front, it had suffered very little from enemy fire.

The "Intelligence" at this time indicated that Prince Rupprecht's great attack might be expected at any moment. The troops in the Salient carried on with their work as if there were no such cloud overhanging them—probably many of them had no inkling of the threatened attack—but the Staff were distinctly "nervy." Raids were carried out every night along our front, and the prisoners obtained always had startling information to give. We were therefore

1918. JUNE.

kept constantly in a state of tension, not knowing what orders the next despatch rider would bring. Several times we were ordered to "stand to" or to "prepare to move at thirty minutes' notice." Extra bandoliers of ammunition were issued to the men, and water-bottles were kept always filled. Very careful plans had been formed, laying down the action of every unit in the Salient in the event of attack.

In spite of all these scares and alarms we managed to enjoy ourselves and carry out some training at Brake Camp. On June 18th we were expecting to be attacked next day, yet in spite of this (or, perhaps, because of it) the men spent a very happy day at that mysterious building known as the "Delousing Station." At night-time we were again ordered to "prepare to move," and all guns in the Salient were moved to different positions awaiting the attack—but eventually we went quietly to bed.

On June 20th we took over the front-line sector south of Hell-fire Corner from the 7th West Ridings. The relief was carried out without any great difficulty, and we settled down to our usual job of improving the trenches. Colonel Branson, who had recovered from his wounds received at Neuve Eglise in April, had now resumed command of the Battalion.

The amount of salvage recovered from this area was tremendous. Whether one needed a porcelain bath or a sack of nails, an armchair or an oil-stove, a brewer's rope or a mail bag, it was easily obtainable—yet the area was hardly a "land flowing with milk and honey." In fact, it stank horribly.

On the night of the 26th the West Yorks. on our left made a raid. The Hun appeared to think it was our fault, and poured literally tons of shells on the Hallamshires' front, fortunately without causing many casualties or doing much damage. Two nights later, at 11-30 p.m., we raided the enemy—or, rather, the enemy's country, for he was nowhere to be found. The raiding party consisted of two companies under Captains Elrington and L. W. Johnson, accompanied by Lieutenant Greenwood and 2nd Lieutenants Jeffs, Foweather and Robins.

Zero hour was fixed for 11-30 p.m., and our artillery put down a terrific bombardment on selected points in the Boche lines.

Our gunners used a good deal of smoke shell, and this would have formed a most effective screen for our men, but just before we went "over" the wind suddenly changed and the smoke screen was blown back in our direction. The smoke "fog" was so thick that it was quite impossible to keep direction or to find anything, and it was difficult to get our men back at all. Even at dawn the following morning it was impossible to see men standing ten feet away. In spite of this *contretemps,* our fellows made a penetration of several hundred yards into the enemy territory, but no one found the enemy except a certain officer who, apparently, caught a Hun, smacked him, and let him go! The Olympians heard our report—and we were ordered to repeat the performance at 11 p.m. next night. Except that the smoke behaved properly and that no Hun was even seen this time, the result was the same—*i.e.,* a blank. There was little doubt that the enemy was holding Cambridge Road as his front line, with merely a scattered post or two in front of it, and, of course, those few poor Huns hurried back to tell their friends when our terrific barrage opened.

After the raid we were relieved in the line by the 5th Y. and L., and went back about two thousand yards to the support area. One company was in a comparatively advanced position at Doll's House, and the remainder of the Battalion some distance behind at Kruisstraat. Mosquitoes in swarms worried us by day and night, and their poisonous bites caused a lot of swollen faces. There was plenty of work to do in this support area, working on our own lines by day, and sending large parties up to work on the front line each night. The monotony of the days was relieved by watching the numerous aeroplane fights, and following the effect of our artillery on the Boche territory in front of us.

Just about this time the Colonel acquired a bright scarlet horsehair fly-whisk, which he always carried on his visits. This whisk was a perfect godsend, as he could be spotted a thousand yards away, and, of course, by the time he reached us, we had set our house in order. General Green-Wilkinson often visited us in the trenches, sometimes accompanied by the Colonel, but more often alone or with a runner. He always carried about with him a cheery "Just had a damned good breakfast" sort of atmosphere, but he had a remarkably keen eye for every detail—"An eye like a plurryawk," as one disgruntled Tommy remarked after the General had passed.

Each morning at about 3 a.m. the enemy opened a barrage, and each one we thought would be THE barrage, but no attack developed. On the night of July 7th we were at last relieved by the 7th West Yorks. We were decidedly thankful, for we had been in the front line for seventeen consecutive days and nights. It was a delight

1918. July.

to get back to Brake Camp, where we remained for eight days' "rest," work on rear defences, and—thank Heaven—bathing.

The 6th Divisional Concert Party, known as "The Fancies," which we had first met in Poperinghe in 1915, were quite close to us, and a large number of officers and men enjoyed their performance each evening. Our own "Tykes" were many miles to the rear at La Lovie Chateau with Divisional Headquarters. We organised several boxing contests on July 14th and 15th, which were enjoyed thoroughly—by the principals as well as the audience.

On the evening of the 15th we marched up to the line again and relieved the 4th West Ridings in the sector immediately north of the Menin Road. The cry of "Wolf" had by this time grown rather monotonous, but information from prisoners told us that the great Boche attack would take place on July 18th, and so we took special precautions to guard against surprises.

Before we had been in the trenches twenty-four hours a full company of American Infantry was sent to us to be "instructed." This company was distributed as follows:—one platoon to each company—one section to each platoon, and the section was then split up amongst the platoon, so that, eventually, each American soldier had two or three British instructors. That was the preliminary lesson of the course, and was known as "Individual Attachment." After a couple of days each American platoon was re-assembled, and although remaining attached each to one of our companies, the platoon acted as a unit under its own commander—"Platoon Attachment." A day later the four American platoons relieved the four platoons of our centre company and held a portion of the front as a company under their own officers, but with one of our companies on each side of them and with a Hallamshire officer left behind with them as guide, counsellor and friend. The next night our B Company returned to the line and relieved the American company, who thereupon marched back to the rear. The whole process was then repeated with another company, and finally the complete American Battalion came up and relieved us in the line—for one night only—after which we returned and the Americans marched to the rear.

Then two companies of another U.S.A. Battalion were sent up to us to be similarly trained, and the "course of instruction," as already detailed, was repeated throughout. The two battalions which we thus instructed were the 2nd and 3rd Battalions of the 118th American Infantry Regiment.

1918. JULY.

As a precaution against the enemy bombardment, which would precede any big attack, the front line trench was vacated every night, and every officer and man moved forward about one hundred yards, so that if the trench had been accurately shelled and blown to bits, the Battalion would have been intact to meet the infantry assault. This was, no doubt, a most excellent plan, but it was aggravating to have to lie out in the slime of "No Man's Land" from midnight to dawn, particularly when it was raining. Many a time on those nights did we pray that the Boche would raid us. He could have hammered our trench for all he was worth without hurting us, and then, when his raiding party came over, expecting to "snaffle" a frightened sentry or two, they would have met, in "No Man's Land," a long line of fixed bayonets. But, of course, the Boche did not provide us with such a pleasant diversion, and so we were compelled to relieve the monotony by "scrounging" for salvage to bring in at dawn.

After the middle of July the Special Company of the R.E. who dealt in "stinks" were thirsting to fire off several hundred bombs filled with a new and very potent gas, but it was essential for the success of the show that the wind should be of a certain speed and blowing in a particular direction. The bombs were all in readiness at the rear, and were to be brought up by a light railway when conditions were propitious for the stunt. Each day we received a code word, which meant that the gas attack would take place, upon which we made our preparations by evacuating a certain sector and bridging trenches—but each evening we received another code word which meant that the operation was postponed. As luck would have it, the wind and atmospheric conditions became favourable on July 23rd, the night that the American Battalion was first left alone in the line. The operations went off with perfect smoothness, and from prisoners' reports afterwards we gathered that the German casualties must have been very great. This gas turned all the green weeds and grass with which "No Man's Land" was covered into a dead brown colour.

On the night of July 28th 2nd Lieutenant Constable and four men went out on an offensive patrol and penetrated several hundred yards into the enemy lines. Large parties of Germans passed quite close to them in the darkness, but no opportunity of securing a straggler presented itself. We therefore prepared a scheme for attempting to capture a few Huns, and this was carried out next day. A party of about twenty-five men, led by 2nd Lieutenants Constable and Jeffs, went into "No Man's Land," in twos and threes, an hour

1918. July.

or so before dusk. They assembled at a spot which Constable knew the enemy occupied at night, and disposed themselves in ambush. The Huns appeared in due course, but, unfortunately, just at that moment our fellows were discovered by an enemy machine-gun post on the flank. There was a general *mêlée,* and our party was driven back under heavy machine-gun fire. We had not secured a prisoner, and had indeed been very fortunate in getting out of such a tight corner with a loss of but three men wounded. In all of these events the American troops had taken the keenest interest, and they were very anxious to try a raid for themselves.

When we finally left them in the line on July 30th we marched back to the line of trenches running through Vlamertinghe known as the "Green Line," and spent the remainder of the night there with Battalion Headquarters in a decrepit farm called Vermouth Villa. In the evening of the last day of July we were relieved by the 6th West Yorks. and marched to Brake Camp.

One of our first duties on arrival at a camp behind the lines was to post anti-aircraft Lewis guns. The necessity for this was proved on our first morning at Brake Camp, when an enemy aeroplane flew low over our area. He was received by a perfect tornado of bullets from our "battery" of four Lewis guns, and the machine at once began to descend, the pilot eventually making a good landing near the Vlamertinghe Road. The Boche airman at once jumped out and ran off in the direction of the front line (four miles away!), but was soon captured. Meantime, a very interesting situation had arisen over the captured aeroplane. British, French and Belgian soldiers surrounded the machine, each claiming it as his prize. It is possible that the 'plane was brought down by our Lewis-gunners, but scores of different people had shot at it, and the incident only terminated when our resourçeful Staff Captain placed a guard over it and declared it a prize of our Brigade. Whether or not this action met with the entire approval of our gallant Allies is unrecorded history.

The next eight days were a pleasant mixture of training and work. On the 5th August all the companies marched up to the "Green Line" defences near Vlamertinghe. Here each company was allotted a definite three-day task, and the men worked to such good purpose that A Company finished its task on the second day, whilst the remaining companies completed theirs early on the third day. The same work, probably, would have taken a week on the old system of making men work for so many hours per day, irrespective of whether they worked well or ill.

In the evening of the 8th August we marched forward again and relieved the 6th West Ridings in the "Brown Line" in support, with Battalion Headquarters at Bobstay Castle. Colonel Branson took over command of the Brigade in the absence of the General, on leave.

For the next eight days we were working on our positions and sending large parties daily to work on Brigade Headquarters at Machine Gun Farm. On the 16th we moved up into the line and relieved the 4th K.O.Y.L.I. in the region of Zillebeke Lake. These were very uneventful days, except that the enemy opened a whirlwind bombardment upon us for a few moments at unexpected times. It was now certain that Prince Rupprecht could not make any great attack on the Ypres Salient, as he had been compelled to send so many of his divisions south. On August 18th our Division was relieved, and the 14th Division (mainly B2 men) took over our sector. Our Battalion was not relieved until 19th August, when the 20th Middlesex took over from us and we returned once again to Brake Camp, arriving at about 3 a.m. on the 20th.

After a day's brushing-up the Battalion moved back by route march to Proven, and was billeted in tents for the night. Many of the officers renewed their acquaintance with old François at the Savoy Restaurant, but we were all quite tired enough to go to bed early. Next morning we marched away at 6 a.m. across the Belgian frontier to Herzeele, a village about twelve kilometres west of Proven. Although we did not know it, we had said our last good-bye to Belgium.

CHAPTER XIV

ARRAS

(See Maps 2 and 4)

DURING our last few weeks in Flanders there had been "a complete change in the whole military situation."

"On the 15th July, the enemy had launched his expected attack east and south-west of Reims, and after making some progress at first and effecting the passage of the Marne, was held by the French, American and Italian forces on these fronts. On the 18th July Marshal Foch launched the great counter-offensive which he had long been preparing on the front between Chateau Thierry and Soissons, supporting this successful stroke by vigorous attacks also on other parts of the German salient. . . . . .

"At a conference on the 23rd July . . . . . the Allied Commander-in-Chief asked that the British, French and American Armies should each prepare plans for local offensives, to be taken in hand as soon as possible, with certain definite objectives of a limited nature. . . . .

"The brilliant success of the Amiens attack was the prelude to a great series of battles, in which, throughout three months of continuous fighting, the British Armies advanced without a check from one victory to another. . . . . ."

Sir D. Haig's Despatch, 21st December, 1918.

The Battalion had spent some days at Herzeele in January, 1916, and the survivors of our original Battalion were delighted to see their old billets again and to renew their acquaintance with the farmers and cottagers of the district after two and a half years. Officers and men were very comfortably billeted, although the Billeting Officer must have been possessed of the imp of mischief when he put the Padre in a very beery estaminet and gave the Quartermaster a room in a convent! Possibly he thought that a little more of the devil in the former and a little more godliness in the latter would be very beneficial all round!

1918. AUGUST—SEPTEMBER.

The Colonel returned from Brigade on August 24th, and on Monday, August 26th, rumours developed into orders. Our transport left at once by road to Renescure, nine kilometres south-east of St. Omer. Early on August 27th the Battalion marched seven kilometres to Rexpoede, and at 2-13 a.m. next day entrained for Petit Houvain, near St. Pol, marching thence to billets at Maisnil—St. Pol and Neuville-au-Cornet, and arriving about 6-30 p.m. after twenty-one hours of travelling. The next day 2nd Lieutenant Teece and thirteen other ranks were returned from the Trench Mortar Battery and at-attached to the Battalion in case of active operations.

In the evening of September 1st we marched a few kilometres to Herlin-le-Sec, travelled by motor lorries to the Chateau de la Haye, and marched to Canada Camp, arriving about 2 a.m. next day. Here the Colonel was summoned to a conference at Brigade Headquarters, and then went up to reconnoitre the sector east of Arras. On his return the usual echelon party was rapidly detailed and despatched to St. Lawrence Camp close by, and the Battalion marched for six hours to the ruined hamlet of Blangy, a couple of kilometres east of Arras, arriving in the small hours of September 3rd.

Here it was billeted in the cellars of ruined houses, and lay down to get what rest it could. The Boche heavies passed over us all the night with a noise like express trains—but they were dropping in Arras, and we were not in Arras. For three days we remained at Blangy, expecting momentarily to be ordered to move up to the front for a battle, but meanwhile doing a little useful training.

At about 7 p.m. on September 5th we were ordered to "about turn," and marched back some twenty kilometres to the village of Gouy-Servins, Battalion Headquarters being accommodated at Petit-Servins near by. The echelon party rejoined us, and we had a solid week of training. On the 11th the Colonel and Company Commanders reconnoitred the forward area, and next day the Battalion marched to Roclincourt, a small village north of Arras. On Friday, the 13th, leaving an echelon party at Mont St. Eloy, we took over the line from the 7th Battalion Black Watch (153rd Brigade) near Gavrelle. The relief was difficult, and was not completed until 6-30 a.m.

The trenches in the sector were in very bad condition, and we were soon literally covered with yellow mud. The enemy held several commanding positions in front of us, and his shelling was often heavy and accurate. On the 17th we provided a large covering party to protect the 5th Y. and L. while they dug a "jumping-off" trench in

1918. SEPTEMBER.

front of our line, and this party came under very heavy machine-gun fire, fortunately with very few casualties. On the previous day we had lost twenty men gassed, but they were able to return to duty after a week or so. We had been doing a little gassing, too—the Special Company R.E. carrying out a successful projector gas attack on our Battalion front at 10-15 p.m. on September 16th.

On September 18th we were relieved by the 5th Y. and L., and took up positions in support. Our five days in the front line had cost us forty-one men—twenty gassed, eighteen wounded, and three killed. One unlucky shell wiped out the whole of A Company's runners, Private Windle being killed and four others wounded.

On the 22nd September the Battalion was very glad to regain Captain P. N. Johnson, M.C., who had been in England since October, 1917.

On the same day the 5th Y. and L. made a successful little attack near Greenland Hill, and we were not surprised when, at 11 p.m. next night, the Boche put down a very heavy barrage on our Brigade front. The S.O.S. was put up, and our counter-barrage came down very promptly. Our troops in the front line opened a heavy rifle and machine-gun fire, and the enemy counter-attack was beaten off. During our time in support we had supplied large working parties, consisting of practically the whole Battalion, to bury cables. The work was similar to that which we did at Vlamertinghe, but not nearly so pleasant, for here we had several hundred men working "on the top" in broad daylight, and within a thousand yards of the front. The work was nearly completed before the enemy balloons spotted us, but then we were given a hot time with eight-inch shells, and the job was finished very much "under fire."

The Battalion was relieved in the afternoon of September 24th by the 7th Argyll and Sutherland Highlanders (51st Division), and trekked across the arid waste of shell-torn earth which had once been Fampoux. A column of motor lorries then carried us to "Y" Camp, a model collection of huts near Etrun, on the Arras—St. Pol. Road, where the echelon party had a hot meal and the mail awaiting us. Here we stayed a fortnight, and carried out some useful training.

As usual, when out of the line for more than a week, we held a Platoon Turn-out Competition—this time Number 1 Platoon (A Company) and the Signallers tied for first place.

The enemy 'planes bombed the surrounding area every night, but the Battalion did not suffer a single casualty from these unpleasant attentions. A huge German bombing 'plane was brought down in flames about 10-30 p.m. on October 5th near our camp.

(a) Avesnes-le-Sec.

At the beginning of October, with the Boche being pushed back everywhere, the Hallamshires expected to be engaged in an attack in the open. Every effort was therefore made to ensure that revenge should be as sweet as possible. Lewis-gun limber-drivers and pack-mule leaders were trained in the use of cover and ground; there were practices in rapid fire, in crossing rivers under fire, attacks in conjunction with artillery, tanks and contact aeroplanes. On the 7th the Division was warned that it would relieve the 2nd Canadian Division—and the chance seemed to have come at last!

On October 8th the Division moved forward. For the Hallamshires the first stage consisted of a three-hour wait by the roadside for 'buses, followed by an uncomfortable journey to Villers Les Cagnicourt, on the Arras—Cambrai road. The Battalion arrived about midnight and bivouacked in the open. On the following afternoon we moved a few miles further east to a similar open space between Marquion and Bourlon.

The forward move of the battle line compelled the relief of the Canadians to be postponed, and on the next day we moved in pursuit, billeting at Faubourg St. Roch, a suburb of Cambrai. The Germans had been driven out of Cambrai only thirty-six hours before our arrival. The buildings in the centre of the town had been blown up or burnt, most of the houses thoroughly ransacked, and all the civilians removed. Numerous booby-traps had been set, and it was pleasing to see Boche prisoners digging up cross-roads to discover possible mines.

By this time the 146th and 147th Brigade had caught up and relieved the Canadians, and on the following morning the 148th Brigade moved out of Cambrai and bivouacked for the night just east of Naves.

The next stage brought us to a desolate spot about three miles from the line, where we again bivouacked. In the course of this march we had the rare and inspiring experience of watching our artillery gallop up to a position at the side of the road, fire rapid for a few minutes, limber up, and continue their journey.

On receipt of a warning that the Brigade would probably attack early the next morning, the C.O. and Company Commanders rode forward to reconnoitre. The line had been reported close up to the river Selle, and it was not until they were fired on by machine guns from high ground near Avesnes-le-Sec while still mounted that the party discovered that the information was quite incorrect, and that the Germans were nearly a mile further west than was expected.

In the meantime, the Corps, acting on an entirely false impression, ordered the barrage for the attack next day to start on the river and to work gradually eastwards. It was apparently impossible to change this plan during the night.

The C.O. received verbal orders for the attack at a conference at Brigade Headquarters, and at about 2 a.m. assembled Company Commanders under a bivouac sheet, explained the objective and boundaries, and issued his own operation orders, the general purport of which was as follows:—

1. The enemy were on the high ground west of the river, and though the Brigade now holding the line had orders to clear the west bank of Germans, if possible, it was likely that opposition would be met before reaching the river.

2. The 5th York and Lancaster Regiment would be on the right of the Hallamshires, the 5th Seaforths (51st Division) on the left, and the 4th K.O.Y.L.I. in Brigade reserve.

3. Our artillery would fire for half-an-hour on the road and railway just east of the river, and would then lift to various strong points behind.

4. B Company would be on the left and would go right through to its final objective. C, on the right, would "mop up" the village of Haspres, and D would "leap-frog" through them at the village. A' would be in reserve, and would move in close touch with Battalion Headquarters, which would be on the Brigade centre line.

5. Zero hour would be 0900 hours. Leading companies were to be ready to move off in artillery formation at 0645, and were to reach the river bank at zero hour.

6. Each company would take seven Lewis guns. Limbers were to unload near Avesnes Station, where an S.A.A. dump would be formed.

The great danger was felt to be that we might find the enemy in large numbers west of the river, where they would be entirely unmolested by our artillery. But for this chance the scheme seemed good.

After a miserably wet night the morning was clear, and as the Battalion moved forward it was difficult to believe that a battle was about to begin. Not a shot could be heard, the village of Avesnes on our left seemed entirely peaceful, though no smoke issued from its chimneys, and there was no sign of trenches or troops. The country is gently undulating, with a fairly well-defined ridge running north and south half a mile or so west of the river, and parallel to it.

As soon as the leading platoons reached this ridge (at about twenty minutes to nine) the enemy sent up his S.O.S. signal. He put a barrage of 77 mm. guns on the ridge and heavily shelled the ground west of Avesnes railway with 5.9's. Immediately a very intense M.G. fire broke out all along the front, and it was very clear that the enemy were in considerable strength west of the river.

The 51st Division could make no progress, and the Hallamshires were, as a result, enfiladed from the left. B and C Companies struggled forward, but began to lose men rapidly, and D met the same fate as they in their turn came over the crest of the hill. The Hun, entirely unmolested by our artillery, had his chance and took it, pouring in a tremendous fire from machine guns and rifles, the volume of which was certainly greater than anything the Battalion had encountered in trench warfare.

At about 9-30 the C.O. ordered A (the support company) forward. Meanwhile, what was left of the other companies had nearly reached the river, but having lost every one of their officers and used most of their ammunition, the survivors were gradually forced back up the hill. A line was taken up on the forward slope, and there at least one counter-attack was beaten off. A Company, no luckier than the rest, soon had all their officers hit, and the M.O. met the same fate. There remained unhurt the C.O., the Adjutant and two subalterns, each of whom was put in charge of half the Battalion.

The experiences of the 5th on our right were very similar, and in the evening the 4th K.O.Y.L.I. relieved the remnants of the two battalions, which then went into support in the open country half a mile or so in rear.

The above shortly describes one of the most disastrous days in the history of the Battalion. No possible fault could be found with the conduct of the Regimental officers and men—indeed, they were much praised by the Corps and Divisional Commanders for the gallantry they displayed—yet the facts that of the 20 officers and 600 men who went into action only 4 officers and 240 men answered the roll next day, and that practically no ground was gained, showed that something had gone very wrong. The explanation is easy.

The British infantryman had once more been ordered to do the impossible. He had gone over the top in broad daylight to attack Germans well entrenched and well supplied with machine guns and artillery. His own artillery gave him no support of any value, for their orders were to fire at points a mile behind the Germans who were doing the damage. No Germans could ever have hoped for a better opportunity of slaughtering Englishmen.

The feelings of the Battalion may easily be imagined. It was certainly difficult to see what reasons High Authority had for thinking on the afternoon of the 12th that there were no Germans west of the Selle, and why, when the true situation was reported in the evening, the artillery programme remained unaltered or the fight was not postponed until the information could be confirmed.

For the next three days the Battalion busied itself cleaning up, re-organising, and making such shelter as was possible with the materials available. The Germans showed no signs of counter-attacking, and the line was fairly quiet. On the 17th the relief of the 49th by the 4th Division began, and after one more night in the open the Brigade returned to Cambrai, where blankets, and billets of a sort, awaited them. The party of officers and men left out of the battle in reserve rejoined, and we were able to re-form the four companies—each, however, consisting only of three weak platoons.

Training began anew, and considerable work was done to improve billets. On the 20th the Prince of Wales visited the Brigade.

If little was achieved on the 13th October, the following list of awards will prove that it was through no lack of effort on the Battalion's part :—

Lieutenant-Colonel D. S. Branson, D.S.O., M.C., was awarded a SECOND BAR to his D.S.O., which was gazetted as follows :—

"For conspicuous gallantry and devotion during the attack on Haspres. After his Battalion had suffered heavy casualties, all the company officers being wounded, he collected the remnants of the Battalion under intense fire, led them forward and consolidated a position. His personal courage and resource were magnificent."

The Military Cross was awarded to Captain W. Ryan and Captain M. Elrington. Of Captain Ryan the Gazette said : "When the leading companies were held up he led his company over the ridge with great skill and dash, and, despite intense machine-gun fire, succeeded in bringing his men almost to the front line. He was then very severely wounded, but he continued to encourage his men and direct their fire until he could be carried away." He lost a leg as a result.

Captain Elrington "carried out his duties as Adjutant with conspicuous success. When there was some doubt as to the exact line held, he made a most daring reconnaissance, going along the whole length of the Battalion front and establishing connection with units on the flank at a time when any movement drew considerable machine-gun fire at close range."

The D.C.M. was awarded to C.S.M. F. Mount, who, "when all officers of his company had become casualties and the attack had been held up, re-organised his men, supervised the consolidation and repeatedly visited the various groups, despite heavy M.G. fire and shelling"; and to Private Jennings, who, whilst acting as Number 1 of a Lewis-gun team, "was hit by a rifle bullet, but carried on. During consolidation he was again hit, but kept his gun in action for another half-hour, until the gun itself was hit and rendered useless."

BARS to the M.M. were given to Corporal C. T. York and Lance-Corporal J. Shepherdson.

Corporal York was sent with his platoon, after his platoon officer and sergeant had become casualties, to reinforce a front line company. "He handled his men skilfully, enabling the company to advance further. He showed such utter disregard for his own personal safety under very heavy M.G. fire that he inspired his men to follow him for a long distance."

Shepherdson took charge of a Stokes-mortar section when its officer had been hit, and led it forward "most gallantly until only himself and one other man were left. He then attached himself to the nearest company, and was of great assistance to the platoon commanders." Later, he helped to bring in the wounded for several hours under continual M.G. fire.

The M.M. was awarded to Sergeants Crossland and Bingham for gallantry and judgment whilst in command of companies after all officers and senior N.C.O.'s had become casualties; and to Corporal Oldfield, Lance-Corporals Ramsden and Davies, Privates Herd, Dawes, Holder, Wolmersley, Bennett and Tate for various acts of gallantry.

(b) The Final Advance.

Meanwhile, the Guards and other Divisions, attacking further south under less unfavourable conditions, had crossed the river Selle, and the Germans had been compelled by the threat to their flank to evacuate the positions between Avesnes-le-Sec and Haspres, where the 49th Division had been held up.

On the 28th the Division again went forward, the Hallamshires moving to Lieu St. Amand, a small village north-west of Avesnes, and thence, two days later, to Haulchin. Here the civilians appeared to be delighted to welcome British troops, and the men were made thoroughly comfortable. The inhabitants were in great want of food and clothing. Soup kitchens were at once formed for them by the British.

November 1st saw the Division again in action at Aulnoy, a small village south-west of Valenciennes, which was captured by the 146th Brigade. Orders for an attack by the 148th Brigade on the following day had been issued and boundaries allotted, but at about midnight, as the Hallamshires were passing through Famars on the way up to the front, these orders were cancelled. We were then ordered to relieve the 5th West Yorks.—further north than we had expected—and an attack was to be made at dawn, with entirely different boundaries and objectives. The relief was completed about 3 a.m., but the attack was postponed at the last moment till 3 p.m.

Meanwhile, strong patrols were pushed out—one discovering that the railway was occupied by enemy M.G.'s, and another rushing an enemy post and capturing twenty prisoners. These reported that Marly was clear, that the enemy was retiring in a north-easterly direction, and that they had previously been manning guns along the railway embankment.

At 3 p.m. A and D Companies were sent forward to establish a line of posts north-east of the Steelworks. The enemy opened a heavy barrage of H.E. on these companies as they were starting, kept up heavy M.G. fire from the village of La Villette, and made some show of resistance at one or two points. The attacking companies, however, advanced to and dug themselves in successfully on the line which had been ordered.

That evening Colonel Branson was wounded by a shell, and was evacuated to England. Major Unsworth took over from him.

On the following day the enemy retired, and the Battalion had no more difficult task than to follow them. This retirement made the front considerably shorter, with the result that the 49th Division were squeezed out of the line and were withdrawn. For them November 3rd was the last day of active operations.

1918. NOVEMBER.

The satisfaction which the Hallamshires felt with this last day of fighting was confirmed in the following awards:—

Military Cross:

Captain R. M. Wilkinson. The success of the attack on the Steelworks "was largely due to the fine example of coolness and courage which he set, and to the skilful way in which he handled his men. While supervising the consolidation of the captured position under heavy shell-fire he was wounded in the face and leg, but although suffering severely from shock and hemorrhage, he refused to leave his company until the Battalion was relieved on the night of 3/4th November."

Distinguished Conduct Medal:

Lance-Corporal J. W. Ayre. When his platoon commander and sergeant had been killed "he took charge of his platoon and continued the advance on the objective. When there, he immediately re-organised his platoon and superintended the consolidation. . . . . . At the moment when he took command the platoon was temporarily checked by a party of the enemy. . . . . . He led the platoon forward, killing or taking prisoners the whole of the party, and capturing a machine gun with its crew."

Military Medal:

Private G. F. Jow, by his prompt and courageous use of a Lewis gun, although he was not a Lewis gunner, enabled his platoon to capture a post (including a machine gun) which was holding up the advance.

A/C.S.M. E. Nash and Sergeant J. Davidson, D.C.M., set fine examples of courage under fire during consolidation.

Private A. Nichols and Private S. Baker did magnificent work in carrying messages under heavy fire.

Bar to the Military Medal:

Private J. Herd did further splendid work with his Lewis gun, engaging an enemy M.G. post and giving valuable covering fire to troops on his right.

On the 4th November we were moved back to Haulchin, and thence, on the following day, to Le Forest. The billets and roads here were dirty, and it took us until Armistice Day to make them presentable.

CHAPTER XV

"APRES LA GUERRE"

WE were resting after that last effort against the Hun near Valenciennes when the order to "down tools" was received. Bursting with energy now, and forgetting the dull and dreary work in the trenches, we were bound to feel a little regret that the joys of the chase should be denied us. There was little room really for regret, however. London and Paris might go mad on Armistice Day, but in Le Forest—a small mining village near Douai—we could appreciate more fully perhaps the lifting of the cloud. "Now we'll get some ruddy sleep o' nights," proclaimed an orderly.

Some of us may have jumped to over-hasty conclusions as to the comfortable effect of the Armistice, but our C.O. foresaw other possibilities! Within a week we began to pride ourselves on our turn-out and ceremonial. Very little escaped Colonel Unsworth, and a whisper was once overheard as he passed down the line: "Our Gerald's got an eye for dirt!"

It was not long before we settled down to the quaint routine of three days' salvage, alternating with three days' ceremonial. All materials of war littered over the country-side had to be collected and dumped. Our area was soon clear, and a morning's salvage developed into a game of "hunt the thimble."

This was not considered a sufficiently instructive or beneficial life for soldiers shortly returning to compete with the workers of civilisation. Education (with a capital E) was launched at us. Apart from "refresher courses" in the "three R's," our ambitious wise men aspired to technical training in every craft—farming, bee-keeping, engineering, and what not.

It would be quite a mistake to suppose that the average man preferred Education to Salvage! But lectures and debate certainly promoted interest, while we were fortunate in having several officers well qualified to instruct and organise classes in many technical subjects.

(a) Raimbeaucourt.

At the end of November, Le Forest being somewhat overcrowded with Brigade Headquarters and the 5th York and Lancaster Regiment, as well as ourselves, we changed our abode to the neighbouring village of Raimbeaucourt. Here we quickly established a strong *liaison* with the French folk, which was happily maintained throughout our stay, though it survived a severe test in January. It was bitterly cold, the fuel ration was short, and wood had to be collected from long distances. Under these conditions we naturally resented the disappearance of our precious goal-posts, 30 yards range, and first-class jumping course!

It was difficult to arouse much interest in education and salvage in the mornings, but the situation was changed in the afternoons. Every day the whole Battalion exercised itself at football chiefly, but also in running, boxing and hockey. Throughout December, January and February we were well represented in every Brigade and Divisional competition. On December 5th we played the R.A.S.C. in the first round of the Divisional Soccer League—a hard game which had to be replayed, resulting in a victory for us. We ultimately reached the final round, in which we were defeated (1-0) by the 6th W. Yorks.

Parallel with our success in games was our improvement at ceremonial, and we felt rather proud of our share in the 49th Divisional Parade on December 16th. The whole of the Division was paraded in line of battalions in column on the fine open ground near Auby. The Army Commander was due to inspect us, but Lieutenant-General Sir A. J. Godley represented him. The "march past" of the gunners at the trot was particularly fine, and three cheers for "Victory" put the finishing touch to an impressive ceremony.

It was on the same day that our first party for demobilisation left. There was much talk and some "grousing" due to the conflicting schemes and orders for demobilisation. Everyone was impatient to be home. "The war was won," it was felt. "We had seen it through. Why sit about in a beastly village of northern France?" This first party consisted of 11 miners, a further 15 went two days later, and by the end of the month some 87 had been dispersed. Matters were certainly a little trying for the majority, who had built high hopes of getting home for Christmas.

Meanwhile, everything possible was done in the way of amusements. The Brigade held a most successful race meeting one afternoon, at which Captain Philip Branson and his *côterie* of horse copers and knaves of the Transport proved themselves as efficient and resourceful as they had always been in more serious competitions versus the Hun, carrying off no less than eleven of the seventeen prizes offered.

1918. DECEMBER—1919. FEBRUARY.

Only a lucky few, of course, could enjoy mounted paperchases and race meetings. For the majority there were, nearly every afternoon, league matches, hare and hounds, baseball and impromptu sports; while the Boche cinema came in handy in the evenings. One end of this theatre was converted into a boxing ring—the scene of much enthusiasm and bloodshed. The question of Christmas dinners, too, afforded opportunity for further enthusiasm, competition and enjoyment.

At the end of December Major R. E. Wilson returned from the Senior Officers' School, Aldershot, and took over the command from Colonel Unsworth.

The procedure of demobilisation became more and more complicated. Few but the unfortunate Demobilisation Officer could keep up with the amazing number of fresh regulations giving priority first to this, and then to that group. The men's case was more direct. Most of them had their "home from home" in the village, and were very "well off," but they felt that those who first entered France should be the first to return to England; and there was scarcely enough work to keep their minds off the one and only subject. Indefinite waiting with little to do is a hard test for any soldier.

On the 9th January Lieutenant Hallam and his party returned from Sheffield with our Colours. The formal reception of these on parade was impressive, and all ranks felt something of the sentiment involved. Though the days of marching into battle with Colours are over, they are still regarded as a sacred charge, and will always retain their value as an emblem of past achievement and future endeavour.

(b) The Rhine.

The month of February was a distinct landmark in the history of the Battalion. It began well, for on the first day we were all more than pleased to welcome back Colonel Branson, full of energy as ever, and apparently none the worse for his wounds. He soon got to the heart of the demobilisation question, and altered our rather perplexed outlook on things in general by a clear and concise exposition of its principles.

Six officers (including Major Unsworth) and 173 men were sent home during the month—a fact which made the outlook far more promising. It was understood, too, on excellent verbal authority, that we were shortly to be reduced to cadre, and would return to Sheffield to make a formal entry and deposit the Colours at Endcliffe Hall. On this understanding some "old hands" volunteered to stay on and risk the postponement of their demobilisation, while the Battalion was content to submit to the ruin of all routine and games.

However, one of life's surprises (without which routine would be deadly) arrived one drowsy Sunday afternoon—in the shape of orders to be in readiness to proceed to Germany AS A BATTALION! Two days later (February 25th) all transport and stores were sent to Douai ready for entrainment. Men eligible for demobilisation were sent to the 5th Y. and L. Regiment for dispersal—and we were left with a total strength of twenty-five officers and 265 other ranks! Most of the latter were youngsters with little or no war service, but we were very glad to have a sprinkling of "old hands" (including Sergeant-Major F. Mount, D.C.M., who became a very efficient and tactful R.S.M.), who had volunteered for the Army of Occupation.

Early on the 26th we paraded at Raimbeaucourt for the last time. It was something of a wrench to leave the comfortable, sleepy village, but we were glad to have the chance of fresh scenery. By 11-30 a.m. all were entrained.

A little anxiety was caused at the start by one half of the train starting without the other, but that was soon allayed. The journey differed little from our experiences on French railways—there were all the usual excitements, stoppages and sudden starts. By 4 a.m. the next day we made Charleroi, where the excellent Halte Repas cheered us on our way with refreshment. At this point our engine driver departed, and no one seemed anxious to take his place. It took eight hours to persuade the Belgian railway officials that we really wanted to continue our journey! After this, we made steady progress, crossing the border into Germany at 8-30 on the morning of the 28th.(1) At 11-30 we detrained at Horrem, marched in the rain to Kerpen, and stayed there the night.

We now came under the command of the 76th Infantry Brigade, 3rd Division. Having been left with only two men and a boy with any transport training, we were naturally not overjoyed at taking over forty-six horses, in addition to the nine we had brought with us! But somehow the T.O. managed to look after them that night, have all the baggage and stores collected next morning, and bring the transport into Cologne in very good order.

(1) Of Officers and Other Ranks who entered France with the Battalion in April, 1915, only three remained to enter Germany with it—Colonel Branson, Captain Philip Branson and R.S.M. Mount. Some 750 of all ranks in the Battalion had given their lives for their Country, whilst the wounded numbered several thousands.

1919. MARCH.

As we approached the Rhineland capital we first saw the twin-spired Cathedral, apparently an immense distance off in the mist, and it seemed an eternity before we entered the town and met Major Wilson with his advance party. From the 1st Battalion Coldstream Guards we took over Rhiel Barracks—in the best quarter of Cologne, and by the river-side. We had never hoped for anything so magnificent!

A good deal of cleaning up was necessary to prepare for an inspection on the 3rd March by General Sir H. Plumer. Our numbers were absurdly small, but he promised an increase to full strength. The fact that we were part of the Army of Occupation meant "something doing" at any rate, and morale was high.

On March 4th we were transferred to the 9th Infantry Brigade, quitting our quarters de luxe for a dirty outlying suburb of Cologne—Ehrenfeld, the entire population of which seemed to live in greatly overcrowded flats. After some pressure and constant use of the interpreter, we managed to find billets, mainly in schools. The delay was trying, as we had preparations to make for a further inspection—this time by Major-General Deverell, C.B.—at 10 the following morning in Blücher Park.

We made another move on the 11th March. The 4th Royal Fusiliers vacated the Nippes area, which adjoined ours at Ehrenfeld, and we were very glad of the chance to take over their billets.

"Anti-fraternising" propaganda by means of lectures, circulars and sermons, backed by stringent standing orders, became a routine to the point of boredom, but without doubt this was the only effective way of frustrating some despicable methods of the "kultured" enemy.

Training was easier to digest. Since the present duty of the Rhine Army was to provide guards throughout the occupied country, our first job was ceremonial. Accordingly for the rest of the month Blücher Park was the *rendez-vous* every morning for all companies, drilling as squad, company or battalion.

Every day now we expected news of reinforcements, and we were very keen to function again as a complete unit. On March 14th we were nearly overwhelmed by two huge drafts, each stronger than ourselves. These were the surplus of two battalions reduced to cadre—13 officers and 276 other ranks from the 2nd Battalion Y. and L. Regiment, and 17 officers with 314 other ranks from our own second line Battalion. As may be imagined, to absorb these in one day was no small task, but re-organisation went smoothly, and in two days the Battalion was ready for inspection by the Brigade Commander—General Potter, C.M.G., D.S.O. The great problem of the occasion was to obtain uniformity, as each draft came with its own "quiffs" in drill!

By this time the red patch at the back of our collars had disappeared, but fortunately Colonel Branson secured the retention of the "Hallamshires" on the shoulders—badges which it is hoped will remain a permanent feature of our dress.

With increased numbers, training assumed a more formidable aspect. There were six hours of education per week, and musketry on ample lines. The excellent Hun ranges at Lachem were allotted to units in turn.

We found a real friend in the Area-Commandant, Major C. Wood—formerly a regular Y. and L. officer. His attitude towards the Huns was delightful, and there was little we lacked that made for our comfort.

At the end of March ten officers left for demobilisation, but few other ranks were now eligible, and we were scarcely prepared for the next surprise. This was the addition of 20 officers and 430 other ranks from the 51st Battalion W. Yorks. Regiment—a "boys" battalion from England. The episode was not a very happy one—we were quite strong enough, and were just beginning to settle down again as a unit; the W. Yorks. had been promised that they should remain as a unit, and on that understanding many of their officers and senior N.C.O.'s had volunteered to stay on. Imagine their bitterness when they were split up after being in Cologne for two days! At the same time a "boys" battalion of the Y. and L. Regiment was absorbed by the 5th and 6th Battalions of the W. Yorks.

On April 12th Lieutenant-Colonel G. B. Wauhope, D.S.O., Y. and L. Regiment, arrived to relieve Colonel Branson, who had decided to return to civil life, but as soon as reorganisation had begun—to conform with the ideas of the new C.O.—Colonel H. R. Headlam, C.M.G., D.S.O., arrived to take over! Thus within four days we had no less than three Commanding Officers! Major Wilson, returning from Paris leave, sought demobilisation. Colonel Wauhope became Second-in-Command, and we soon settled down again. The regularity of leave helped. Officers went every three or four months; the men every five or six months. The train service was excellent, special

1919. MAY.
Cologne—Boulogne expresses being run in conjunction with the Channel boats.

During May guard duties were increased considerably, but the system was improved. Instead of finding a few guards each, battalions now supplied all the Brigade duties for a week at a time. The principal guards were at Langerich and Cologne docks—a whole company being allotted to each. The Cologne Dock guard was quite interesting, as frequent attempts were made by civilians to steal the food and stores deposited there. We were successful in catching and bringing to trial some half-dozen miscreants. The other guard was away in uninteresting country, and very lonely. In this case a huge concrete ammunition park, with some captured guns and other war material, was our charge. There were one or two attempts to steal stores, and once a serious fire was caused by some Bolshevists, though this was not during our tour of duty. A sentry of ours was wounded on one occasion, but the offender could not be traced.

May brought two incidents of interest to all in Cologne. On the 16th we took part in the very impressive welcome given to Marshal Foch. The effect of this stirring personality on the Huns was most marked. They obviously stood in awe of the soldier whose brain and courage had defeated their Imperial War Lords. Many rumours were current at this time to the effect that the French would occupy Cologne in place of the British. That was the last thing the civilians wanted!

On the following day we enjoyed an excellent steamer trip up the Rhine at the Huns' expense—our first experience of the kind. Our next was two months later, and was even more delightful, as we took the train to Bonn, itself well worth a visit, and then the steamer right up to Coblentz.

At this time our huge numbers began to be reduced. The various departmental corps were very short of men owing to demobilisation, and we had to send fifty to the R.A.M.C., fifty to the R.A.S.C., and one hundred and sixty to the 52nd Battalion Northumberland Fusiliers at Rhiel Barracks.

(c) Peace.

There was much delay and doubt before Peace was signed on the 23rd June. Feeling ran high in Cologne, where all the civilians were more than anxious for peace at the earliest possible moment, while some of us thought the Hun should be taught a lesson, and not merely dismissed with a caution. On the 16th June we received orders to be ready to advance by march route to a bridge-head twenty miles east of Cologne, where we should be in a position to jump off the mark if the Germans failed to sign.

On the morning of the 18th the advance was begun, the first day's trek being only as far as Dunwald, where the Brigade bivouacked for the night. Early next morning the march was resumed, and our destination was reached about 2 p.m. This was the hottest day of the year, and we were not sorry to doff our packs and find snug billets at Hilgen. Here we remained in comfort, and awaited the momentous decision.

There was perhaps a slight wave of disappointment when Peace had been actually signed. The prospect of going further into Germany was a tempting one to some of us. We stayed on at Hilgen, however, till the end of the month. The surrounding country, made up of wonderful hills and deep valleys, well wooded and dotted with small lakes and reservoirs, was ideal for field training—a fact which was not lost on our C.O., who originated some very interesting Battalion schemes.

Colonel Wauhope left at this time to command another battalion, and his place was taken by Major V. T. R. Ford, D.S.O., Y. and L. Regiment, whom all ranks soon took to their hearts.

At the end of June, with great reluctance, we returned to our billets in Nippes. Those ten days in the country made a welcome break in the routine of the town. The improvement in the men's health and appearance was very marked, and they returned to Cologne bronzed, fit, and full of energy.

Before resuming guard duties, we took part in two very interesting ceremonial shows. On July 6th General Gouraud, a famous Frenchman who lost his arm in the war, paid a visit to Cologne, and we were detailed for the guard of honour. Colonel Headlam was in command of the whole parade. The Hallamshires, under Major Ford, were lined up with their backs to the Cathedral steps; cavalry, gunners and marines formed the other three sides of the square. General Gouraud, accompanied by General Sir W. Robertson, then Commanding the Rhine Army, inspected the guard of honour, and appeared well pleased with his reception. A "march-past" in column of fours completed the ceremony.

The next event involved several strenuous practices. This was the visit of Mr. Winston Churchill and the Army Council. The whole of the VIth Corps was paraded at Lachem. The programme was elaborate—it may suffice to say that everything went well, and that several of the spectators told us afterwards that the Hallamshires were second to none in the "march-past."

August brought another change in command. Though sorry to lose him, we had to congratulate Colonel Headlam on his appointment as G.S.O.I. at Simla. Before he left, however, he secured the appointment of Major Ford as his successor. With this the Battalion was well pleased. Major Vanderzee, from the 5th W. Yorks., was posted as Second-in-Command, and proved a good friend to the Battalion. Guard duties now became more onerous, as the 5th W. Yorks. were sent into the country on police duty.

From the signing of Peace, Cologne became very gay. Officially, the restrictions in regard to fraternising were removed, but very few wanted to associate with the Huns. Every afternoon and evening there was a wide choice of entertainment and recreation.

The Rhine Army Sports Club was formed, and, after taking over the best tennis courts, it proceeded to make cricket and hockey pitches in the Huns' favourite park at Lindenthal. In September cricket came to an end, our First XI. finishing 4th in the Cologne Cup matches. Football began again, and we were very proud of our first serious attempt at hockey—winning every match except one, which was a draw.

In the town itself dances, theatres, concerts and cinemas drew "full-houses." The Cologne Dramatic Society, run by Lieutenant Percy, gave excellent performances (mostly light plays and farces) nearly every evening.(1) The British Empire Leave Club was very popular among the men for dances and concerts. Our amusements, as much as anything else, were very cheap, as the mark gradually decreased as low as 200 to the pound sterling.

It was unfortunate that so few of those present with the Battalion had seen active service, and therefore failed to appreciate to the full the ease and comfort of their lot.

(d) "Home, Sweet Home."

As soon as Peace was signed, little time was lost in reducing the Rhine Army. The first step was to demobilise all men who had originally attested voluntarily. This reduced our numbers to 34 officers and 390 Other Ranks, and necessitated a further re-arrangement of billets. Nussbaumer Schools became Headquarters, and two

(1) Colonel Ford played several parts.

1919. NOVEMBER.

companies moved to Bickendorf — a dirty, overcrowded neighbourhood, where the civilians were inclined to insolence.

All regular units had left in June for re-forming in England prior to foreign service, and we therefore expected that 1st Line Territorial Battalions would be the next for home, although many rumours were rife, as usual.

On November 3rd a preliminary order was received to be ready to move either as a battalion or as a cadre. This sounds simpler than it was in practice, as there were vastly different sets of regulations for battalions and cadres—the chief difficulty in the latter case being the disposal of transport and surplus stores. However, three days later a definite order was received to reduce to cadre strength forthwith.

Orderly Room and Quartermaster's Stores were worked at very high pressure, and the Battalion shed its transport vehicles, horses, stores and equipment in a marvellously short time. Men who had volunteered for the Rhine were sent to a Rest Camp to await transfer to various units; but cadre strength is five officers and fifty other ranks. What were we to do with the remaining two hundred and forty other ranks—young soldiers and conscripted men? At the last moment an order came to demobilise them immediately, regardless of the nature or date of their attestation. This was a very quick, though scarcely judicious, solution to the muddle. There were men in other units far more eligible—and the expressions on the faces of the fortunates when they paraded for dispersal were amusing, showing at the same time utter surprise, joy, and suspicion of a catch somewhere! The question of officers was easy, as they were all volunteers for the Army of Occupation, and were transferred to the 51st Battalion N.F.'s for police duty in outlying districts.

The cadre left Cologne under the Adjutant on November 8th. General Potter, his staff, and those remaining behind, gave the party an excellent send-off; and the weather expressed its grief with tears. The movement of troops at the time was enormous, so that "grousing" was unreasonable, but the forty-eight hours' journey to Calais in leaky cattle-trucks was far from pleasant. Luckily, our men only had to wait twenty-four hours in the Rest Camp, and at 9 a.m. on the 11th were well out of Calais Harbour. Exactly a year after the signing of the Armistice the Battalion's work in the war, and its aftermath, came to an end; and it was indeed a striking fact that the two minutes' silence was observed just as the boat was made fast to the wharfside at Dover.

1919. NOVEMBER.

The party reached London about 5 p.m.—too late to go on to Sheffield, and it was decided to quarter at Victoria for the night. This afforded a useful opportunity for giving buttons and brasses a polish—very much needed after cattle-trucks, Rest Camp, mud, and continuous rain. Colonel Branson met the party next morning and travelled with it to Sheffield. On arrival there at 12-15 p.m. it was given a tremendous reception.

*   *   *   *   *   *

It is impossible to record faithfully the feelings of those tense moments. The strength of the Cadre seemed to suggest the fact that many brave Hallamshires would never return to Sheffield; but as the Colours were put away at Endcliffe Hall that Cadre could well feel that it represented "something accomplished." Appreciation of that fact by Higher Authorities will have been found in the foregoing pages; it was not lacking in the citizens of Sheffield on that 12th day of November, 1919.

APPENDIX

Decorations awarded to Officers, N.C.O.'s and Men for service with the Hallamshires. Names are given by ranks in alphabetical order, and the rank shewn is the highest acting or permanent rank held with the Battalion, so far as it has been possible to ascertain.

Rank.	Name.	Decorations, etc.
Lt.-Col.	D. S. Branson	D.S.O. Bar to D.S.O. 2nd Bar to D.S.O. M.C. Five times mentioned in despatches.
Lt.-Col.	G. Unsworth	M.C.
Lt.-Col.	R. E. Wilson	M.C. Bar to M.C.
Lt.-Col.	L. J. Wyatt	D.S.O. Twice mentioned in despatches.
Major	M. J. Duggan	Mentioned in despatches.
Major	E. M. Holmes	M.C.
Major	J. E. D. Stickney	Mentioned in despatches.
Captain	H. G. Barber	M.C. Mentioned in despatches.
Captain	C. A. Bernard, R.A.M.C.	M.C.
Captain	P. A. Branson	Mentioned in despatches.
Captain	S. Brooke	M.C. Mentioned in despatches.
Captain	M. Elrington	M.C.
Captain	D. P. Grant	M.C.
Captain	L. W. Johnson	M.C.
Captain	P. N. Johnson	M.C. Twice mentioned in despatches.
Captain	J. L. Marsh	Mentioned in despatches.
Captain	H. Payne	M.C.
Captain	W. Ryan	M.C.
Captain	W. Tozer	Mentioned in despatches.
Captain	R. M. Wilkinson	M.C.
Captain	R. M. Williams	M.C. Mentioned in despatches.
Captain	H. K. Wilson	Mentioned in despatches.
Captain	J. F. Wortley	M.C. Mentioned in despatches.

APPENDIX

Rank.	Name.	Decorations, etc.
Lieutenant	W. D. G. Gifford	M.C. Bar to M.C.
Lieutenant	A. Gladwin	Mentioned in despatches.
Lieutenant	T. E. Sanderson	Mentioned in despatches.
2nd Lieutenant	E. S. Christmas	M.C.
2nd Lieutenant	W. Constable	M.C.
2nd Lieutenant	C. R. Hope	M.C.
2nd Lieutenant	S. E. Warburton	M.C., M.M.
R.S.M.	G. Imisson	M.C. D.C.M. M.M. Belgian Croix de Guerre Mentioned in despatches.
R.S.M.	F. Mount	D.C.M.
R.S.M.	W. Sykes	Twice mentioned in despatches.
R.Q.M.S.	H. Cole	Mentioned in despatches.
R.Q.M.S.	H. Thickett	M.S.M.
C.S.M.	W. Cadman	D.C.M. Mentioned in despatches.
C.S.M.	W. Hall	Mentioned in despatches.
C.S.M.	W. S. Hutchinson	D.C.M.
C.S.M.	E. Nash	M.M.
C.S.M.	G. Pearson	D.C.M.
C.S.M.	W. Pemberton	D.C.M., M.M.
C.S.M.	W. Wagg	D.C.M.
C.S.M.	W. Wood	D.C.M., M.M. Belgian Croix de Guerre. Mentioned in despatches.
C.Q.M.S.	F. Goodwin	M.S.M.
Sergeant	F. Baker	M.M.
Sergeant	G. H. Beedham	D.C.M.
Sergeant	A. Bingham	M.M.
Sergeant	G. A. Brown	M.M.
Sergeant	T. W. Cartwright	M.M.
Sergeant	A. W. Clarke	D.C.M.
Sergeant	J. Davison	D.C.M., M.M.
Sergeant	W. R. Dodd	M.M.
Sergeant	C. Firth	D.C.M.
Sergeant	E. Greaves	M.M.
Sergeant	A. Jones	D.C.M.
Sergeant	J. Kay	M.M.
Sergeant	L. Lawless	D.C.M.
Sergeant	R. Megson	D.C.M.
Sergeant	W. H. Naylor	Mentioned in despatches.
Sergeant	G. A. Shute	D.C.M.
Sergeant	P. Skelton	Mentioned in despatches.
Sergeant	J. E. Warren	M.M.
Sergeant	E. White	M.S.M. Mentioned in despatches.

APPENDIX

Rank.	Name.	Decorations, etc.
L/Sergeant	F. Crossland	M.M.
L/Sergeant	W. D. Galley	M.M.
Corporal	A. Eaton	M.M.
Corporal	S. Fell	M.M.
Corporal	H. Green	M.M.
Corporal	T. F. Hayes	M.M.
Corporal	G. Hudson	M.M.
Corporal	F. Lupton	M.M.
Corporal	H. Oldfield	M.M.
Corporal	A. Waters	M.M.
Corporal	H. Wilkinson	D.C.M.
Corporal	C. T. York	M.M.
		Bar to M.M.
L/Corporal	J. W. Ayre	D.C.M., M.M.
L/Corporal	J. Barlow	Mentioned in despatches.
L/Corporal	H. Bathe	M.M.
L/Corporal	J. W. Biggin	D.C.M.
L/Corporal	E. Bower	M.M.
L/Corporal	J. Brady	M.M.
L/Corporal	C. Brown	M.M.
		Mentioned in despatches.
L/Corporal	W. T. Coote	D.C.M.
L/Corporal	A. Crapper	D.C.M.
L/Corporal	W. E. Davies	M.M.
L/Corporal	W. Fell	M.M.
		Mentioned in despatches.
L/Corporal	A. Foster	M.M.
L/Corporal	G. Freeman	M.M.
L/Corporal	T. Hall	M.M.
L/Corporal	M. Jackson	D.C.M.
L/Corporal	C. Lawrence	M.M.
L/Corporal	H. Leaver	M.M.
L/Corporal	F. Leggatt	D.C.M.
L/Corporal	H. Levesley	M.M.
L/Corporal	G. Lindley	M.S.M.
L/Corporal	H. Marton	D.C.M.
L/Corporal	C. Ogden	M.M.
L/Corporal	H. C. Porter	M.M.
L/Corporal	H. Ramsden	M.M.
L/Corporal	A. G. Scarbrooke	M.M.
L/Corporal	A. P. Tarlton	M.M.
Private	A. Adley	M.M.
Private	J. Andrews	M.M.
Private	H. Atkinson	M.M.
Private	S. Baker	M.M.
Private	L. Barron	M.M.
Private	A. Bennett	M.M.
Private	T. E. Bennett	M.M.
Private	A. B. Cahill	M.M.

APPENDIX

Rank.	Name.	Decorations, etc.
Private	J. Clark	M.M.
Private	B. S. Coulson	M.M.
Private	J. Cowlishaw	D.C.M.
Private	R. Crow	Mentioned in despatches.
Private	F. Dale	M.M.
Private	W. E. Davies	M.M.
Private	Dawes	M.M.
Private	G. Downes	M.M.
Private	C. Dungworth	M.M.
Private	E. Gray	M.M.
Private	A. Gunn	M.M.
Private	J. Herd	M.M. Bar to M.M.
Private	W. R. Holder	M.M.
Private	E. Hopkinson	M.M. Bar to M.M.
Private	S. Ibbotson	M.M.
Private	H. Jeffery	M.M.
Private	J. Jelley	M.M.
Private	P. Jenkinson	M.M.
Private	J. H. Jennings	D.C.M.
Private	G. F. Jow	M.M.
Private	F. Lockwood	M.M.
Private	J. Longden	M.M.
Private	F. Lymer	M.M.
Private	R. Mackie	M.M.
Private	W. E. Marshall	M.M.
Private	T. McAvoy	M.M.
Private	A. Morton	M.M.
Private	A. H. Neve	M.M.
Private	A. Nichols	M.M.
Private	H. Peart	M.M.
Private	A. Peat	M.M.
Private	V. Rogers	M.M.
Private	F. W. Sissons	M.M.
Private	J. Smith	M.M.
Private	T. Tate	M.M.
Private	G. Thickett	M.M.
Private	T. Thickett	D.C.M.
Private	C. Turtle	M.M. Bar to M.M.
Private	W. Tyler	M.M.
Private	A. Vernon	M.M.
Private	F. W. Wharton	M.M.
Private	T. K. Wilson	M.M.
Private	R. Winter	M.M.
Private	G. H. Wolmersley	M.M.
Private	P. Wray	M.M.

INDEX